D0176018

FabJob Guide to

Become a Professional Organizer

Grace Jasmine
and Jennifer James

FABJOB® GUIDE TO
BECOME A PROFESSIONAL ORGANIZER
by Grace Jasmine and Jennifer James

ISBN-13: 978-1-894638-66-1
ISBN 10: 1-894638-66-2

Library and Archives Canada Cataloguing in Publication

Jasmine, Grace
FabJob guide to become a professional organizer /
Grace Jasmine and Jennifer James

Includes a CD-ROM.
Includes bibliographical references.
ISBN-13: 1-894638-66-1
ISBN-10: 1-894638-66-2

1. Organization—Vocational guidance. 2. Home economics—Vocational guidance. I. James, Jennifer. II. Title. III. Title: Become a professional organizer
TX147.J38 2005   640   C2005-902959-5

FabJob Inc.
19 Horizon View Court
Calgary, Alberta, Canada T3Z 3M5

FabJob Inc.
4616 25 Avenue, NE
Seattle, Washington, USA 98105

To order books in bulk, phone 403-949-2039
To arrange an author interview, phone 403-949-4980

www.FabJob.com

About the Author

Grace Jasmine, an award-winning author and business owner, has a deep appreciation of the professional organizing industry. In a writing career spanning the last 15 years, Grace has researched and written more than 40 books, a feat made possible by carefully and effectively organizing her ideas and her time.

As a career counselor, Grace has also helped clients organize their goals, job searches, and professional approaches. By helping define and create steps to professional success, she has moved hundreds of people like you closer to realizing their dreams.

For this guide, Grace met with and interviewed the many professionals who work in the organizing industry, in order to provide first-hand insider information for you in this authoritative how-to book.

About the Editor

Jennifer James leads the Editorial Department at FabJob Inc., the world's leading publisher of information about dream careers. She has edited, researched for, and contributed to more than 30 FabJob career guides, including lead writing credits on the *FabJob Guide to Become a Makeup Artist* and the *FabJob Guide to Become a Fashion Designer*. She is the former editor of a national sports publication, and studied journalism at Ryerson University in Toronto.

Acknowledgements

Naturally, a book like this requires the expert knowledge of talented and experienced individuals. I would like to thank the Arizona chapter of the **National Organization of Professional Organizers** for so graciously welcoming me to their events and meetings, and presenting themselves as a unified expression of goodwill and know-how.

I am grateful to **Barry Izsak**, president of the National Association of Professional Organizers (NAPO) and owner of Arranging It All in Austin, Texas, and **Laurene Livesey Park**, past president of Professional Organizers of Canada (POC) and owner of Organize Me 101 in Ontario, Canada, who were both kind enough to share their valuable insights about the industry.

Additionally, the friendly wisdom and real-life experience of the many successful professional organizers who were willing to share their stories have added invaluably to this text. These professional organizers, and the companies they own, are:

- **Brenda Clements**, Complete Organizational Services; Glendale, Arizona

- **Ramona Creel**, OnlineOrganizing.com; Atlanta, Georgia

- **Carol Halsey**, Business Organizing Solutions; Wilsonville, Oregon

- **Rozanne Hird**, R R Hird & Company; Phoenix, Arizona

- **Chris McKenry**, Get It Together LA!; Los Angeles, California

- **Marcy Tanner**, Organized and Successful; Phoenix, Arizona

- **Karen Ussery**, Organized for Success; Phoenix, Arizona

The editors thank the following companies (listed alphabetically) for providing product photos for this book: **California Closets**, **Mill's Pride**, **Stacks and Stacks**, and **Staples**.

Contents

Classic White bedroom walk-in closet. © 2005 California Closet Co. Inc. All Rights Reserved.

1. Introduction

Welcome to the world of professional organizing!

Perhaps since the first day you realized you had a knack for organizing, you have been dreaming about a way to put your talents to good use. You love to create functional and beautiful surroundings and you always seem to know just how to improve the way tasks are completed and things are done. You have always thought it would be wonderful to be your own boss.

Being a professional organizer allows you to use your talents to teach others to get their lives in order. You will help people live personal and professional lives full of peace, beauty, and most importantly, organization!

As a buyer of this book, you probably got here one of two ways. Either you have always been passionate about order and have a talent for organizing things that began as early as you can remember, or you had an organizational "metamorphosis" in which you suddenly realized that the chaos and the clutter in your life was hurting you, and you changed.

However you got here, there is wonderful news. Even if you have never organized anyone but yourself, you can learn how to be a professional organizer. And there has never been a better time to pursue this career. You have chosen a rapidly growing and relatively young profession that continues to change and progress.

This guide will take you from the first moment you realize you have the organizational skills to create your own business, to the day you have a schedule full of appointments with clients who rely on you to help them get their lives, their homes, and their businesses organized to perfection.

We'll start by introducing you to the job a professional organizer does. And why would someone want to organize for a living? You'll find out about the many benefits of this exciting new career that is attracting thousands of new people every year.

1.1 What is a Professional Organizer?

A professional organizer is an individual who helps other people get organized for a living. You will apply your advanced understanding of organizational systems and processes to other people's chaotic situations, and help them develop solutions that work in their lives. So essentially, you are a professional troubleshooter and problem-solver. In many cases a professional organizer is also a:

- Consultant

- Counselor

- Information systems expert

- Home economist

- Office manager

- Teacher

- Time management coach

- Space designer

- Speaker

If this list looks a little daunting right now, you will soon begin to see that many of these skills are untapped and unrefined skills that you already possess. Others can be learned with a little study and practice, which this guide will lead you through.

A Typical Day

A typical day for a professional organizer can be many things — or anything he or she chooses. They are the ultimate organizational entrepreneurs. On the job, they are often working hands-on with clients who need their help to get their lives, their homes, and their businesses organized.

As you'll read more about later, people hire organizers to help with things like choosing, purchasing, and installing organizing equipment (filing cabinets, storage containers, racks, etc.), designing time schedules that help them get things done, sorting out files on a computer that have gotten overwhelming, purging an overgrowth of knick-knacks, paper, and other clutter from room to room, or developing systems that maximize the use of time and resources on a personal or business level.

Depending on your specialty, you might be the one to physically rearrange furniture and computer files, or you might simply provide your knowledge and give your clients systems they can implement themselves. You offer guidance, support, and you might even hold the garbage bag! Professional organizers also spend their days:

- Thinking about organizational challenges

- Listening to clients

- Creating solutions with tools and ideas

- Communicating organizational concepts to clients

- Planning organized systems

- Testing and refining new ideas

- Meeting people and explaining what they do

- Making a difference to their clients

There are so many different ways to be a professional organizer that you can easily refine your own skills to create the sort of business that fits you, your strengths, and your personality. If you have the desire to help people get organized in their homes and businesses, you can learn to be a professional organizer.

A Not-So-Typical Day

Professional organizers are people with motivation and passion about what they do. Quite often they are designing their careers as they go along. You have the luxury of making your business as unique as you want it to be. The organizers interviewed for this book have taken their careers in specialized directions that might be of interest to you too. For example:

- If you are **Barry Izsak**, you might spend your day developing training and education programs for other organizers.

- If you are **Carol Halsey**, you might be talking to clients internationally, or sending your published tip book out in boxes of hundreds to buyers.

- If you are **Laurene Livesey Park**, you might be co-authoring a book on organizing, or talking on the radio.

- If you are **Chris McKenry**, you might be facilitating a workshop or speaking at a civic group.

- If you are **Rozanne Hird**, you might be representing yourself and your company at an important charity event.

1.2 Benefits of the Career

Being a professional organizer is the perfect way for you to be in control of your life, your time, and your income. Here are some of the many benefits you can expect in this fabulous career… and no doubt, you will discover many more on your own.

Help People Live Better Lives

Do you love helping people? Are you someone who really likes the feeling of making an important difference in the lives of others? Being a professional organizer will allow you to make a profound impact on the lives of your clients on a daily basis. People will often think of you as the person who literally "saves" them from a wide variety of problems. Many times clients call an organizer when they feel they are in organizational trouble. You will be the person that helps them to make things right again.

Getting a chance to share your knowledge with people who pay for it, thank you for it, and actually think it is vital to them, is a huge gift. Professional organizers agree that what they do makes an important difference to people, and they get frequent feedback that their clients appreciate their advice and knowledge.

Work at What You Love

One of the most amazing things about becoming a professional organizer is that you will have the opportunity to do what you love all day long, every day, and get paid for it. Most professional organizers agree that it is extremely fulfilling to get paid for something they love to do anyway — create order.

You have the freedom to design a business based on your strengths. Are you great at developing filing systems? Then you might focus on helping those with home or small businesses. Are you someone who likes to work with seniors? Then you might focus on helping seniors move into retirement housing. Are you someone who loves to cook and understands how to make a kitchen into a beautiful and well-functioning place? Then kitchen space design might be your specialty.

As a professional organizer, what you do best becomes the focal point of your business.

Be Your Own Boss

Have you always dreamed that one day you would work for yourself? Have you always wanted to have more control over your career — and actually be in charge of how things turn out? Being in control of your daily work decisions and the long-term outcome of your professional life is something you have to look forward to.

Be Seen as an Expert

As a professional organizer, you become an authority about your business. People will look to you for advice and hire you to solve their problems at home and in the workplace. As you build your business and help your clients find solutions to their organizing dilemmas, word will travel and your popularity and reputation will increase.

You will get a chance to interact with members of your community as you develop a professional network. Professional organizers find that networking and public speaking are some of the most important ways to make contacts and gather new clients. As you develop a flair for public speaking, you will find that you may become known in your own area, and certainly in your business community.

Some professional organizers are sought-after speakers, are regularly asked for interviews for magazine and newspaper articles, and appear on local radio and television shows.

Create Beauty and Order

As a professional organizer, you will get a chance to use and explore your sense of beauty. The most successful organizers talk about how they not only create functional spaces, but also beautiful ones for their clients to use and enjoy. If you have always been told you have a "good eye" or a "flair" for making things work efficiently, as well as look good, your talent will have a home in this career.

Meet New Challenges

Do you have a knack for systems? Are you someone who sees a problem and immediately find yourself brainstorming potential solutions? As a professional organizer, your ability to problem-solve and develop systems will be sought after. Your ability to create order out of chaos will be in high demand.

1.3 In This Guide

By purchasing this guide, you have taken the first step in making your dream of becoming a professional organizer a reality. In the pages that follow, you will find out exactly what you need to do to turn your passion for order into a successful business. You will learn how to package and market the skills you already have, and how to acquire the skills that may be new to you.

Chapter 2 (*The World of Organizing*) starts by examining the roots of this industry, from home economics to industrialization to downsizing in the workplace, and their effects on organization as a concept. Then we take a closer look at where it has all led to: professional organizing as a career. You'll read about the characteristics organizers share, the many hats they wear to serve their clients' needs, and areas you can specialize in.

Chapter 3 (*How to Organize*) will teach you how to organize anything, using proven systems and strategies. It begins with an awareness of what it means to organize. You'll be introduced to the five key principles organizers use to create order. Once you understand the systems, then we'll apply them to the different environments you might choose to work in: personal, residential, and business. We'll take you through each of these specializations step-by-step and room by room, with helpful checklists and forms you'll be able to adapt for use with your own clients.

In Chapter 4 (*Starting an Organizing Business*) you will learn how to set up your organizing business. You'll assess your skills and be given resources to tap into to help you become an industry expert. Then you'll get detailed instruction on how you set up and run an organizing business, from planning to licenses to bookkeeping to setting your fees. You'll be amazed at how inexpensive and simple it really is to get started.

In Chapter 5 (*Marketing and Sales*) you will learn more about the heart of any successful business: effective marketing and sales techniques. Our experts have shared their insider tips on how they grew their start-ups into successful organizing businesses, through getting the word out cheaply and effectively with tip books, articles, public seminars, and more. With potential clients calling, the next thing you'll learn is how to sell your services like a pro… and then how to close the deal.

Finally, Chapter 6 profiles some successful professional organizers to inform and inspire you, and gives you local association contacts and vital industry resources that will help you get started as a professional organizer right away.

Throughout the guide and on the CD-ROM that accompanies this book, look for important forms and checklists that will help you successfully organize, run, evaluate, and enhance your business. By moving through the information in the following chapters, you will find that you are soon ready to be a professional organizer!

2. The World of Organizing

"For me being organized isn't a choice, it's a necessity."

— Barry Izsak, Professional Organizer

Just like any other profession that you might decide to get involved in, there are some basics you will need to learn to get an overview of the professional organizing industry.

By the time you are finished with this chapter, you will have a good basic knowledge of the professional organizing industry. This chapter gives a history of the industry, identifies characteristics of successful professional organizers, and describes areas you can specialize in.

2.1 The History of Organizing

From the day prehistoric people first used the same tool twice, they began to create order. The simple fact that someone placed a tool where it could be found for a second time meant that a system had been created —something was put in a place where it could be found and used again.

Since people began to gather in units or families to work together to do what was necessary every day to survive, they have been organizing their space. To organize, by definition, means to put things in order, to sort out or arrange things, or to systemize.

Prior to the early 1980s, professional organizing as an industry really wasn't on the map, according to industry expert Barry Izsak. Changing personal needs and trends in living and in business have created a niche for those who can organize.

Home Economics

> *"Homemaking today should have a background of scientific training. The average girl wants to be able to keep her house with the least possible strain, and in order to do this she must have good training… best achieved by taking a good course in home economics."*

— Eleanor Roosevelt, 1933

As early as 1868, "home economics" courses were taught at Iowa State College. The idea of home economics was based on the theory that the practice of homemaking should be elevated to a science. By applying the principles of science and management to the practice of home arts, it was thought they could be made more efficient.

The field of home economics eventually became known as the field of family or human ecology, which today comprises a far wider reaching and in-depth look at family and home sciences. Courses at universities today include topics like Human Factors and Interior Space, and Space Planning and Programming.

Scientific Management

What organizers do today began with the advent of the field of scientific home management. The forerunners of this profession were the first individuals to realize that the effective functioning of the home environment could be planned, thoughtfully organized, and executed according to a system. Two individuals were forerunners in the concepts of scientific management — Frederick Winslow Taylor and Henry L. Gantt.

The principles of scientific management were first developed by Frederick Winslow Taylor (*1856–1915*). Taylor was the first person to set performance standards, investigate and determine what a full day's standard work was, conduct time studies in the work place, and to break down large jobs into smaller tasks, what he called "task management."

Henry L. Gantt (*1861–1919*) is most famous for his invention of the Gantt chart, in which he invented a way to plan and show work over time (you'll learn later how to use these charts to help your clients). Gantt's theoretical inventions moved the concepts of time management, project management, and workflow forward in industry.

Professional organizers who work today in corporate settings benefit from the early work in the theory and practices of scientific management. The ability to review systems, procedures, and processes, and make recommendations for improvement is an extension of the exploration and application of the theoretical investigations that began with Taylor in the 19th century.

Other Contributing Factors

Part of the need for professional organizing today is due to how our world has changed in the last few hundred years. Here are some of the major factors that have contributed towards creating this niche.

Industrialization

The history of organizing the workplace truly began around the time of the industrial revolution, when the advent of the factory and the need to manage the work that went on there were the catalysts for the trends in thought that eventually led to scientific management. Once factories were established, workers came to work in them, and the need for a way to organize or manage these workers and the tasks they did evolved.

Management was needed to determine the processes and systems by which workers would do the tasks necessary to manufacture goods. Issues of production, labor, training, and development of systems and procedures became important to the successful operation of factories.

Nesting

Around the late 1980s "nesting" became a societal rage. The societal trend of nesting – that is, focusing on and creating a cozy, and highly useable, living space to retreat to from the hassles of the rest of the world – is another reason for the increase in the numbers and popularity of professional organizers.

People need help preparing and organizing their "nests," according to organizing expert Karen Ussery. People driven by their intense work lives and corporate climbs look to their downtime as a time to settle into their homes and commune with a small circle of family and friends.

Add to this societal phenomenon forerunners in the industry like Martha Stewart, and suddenly being in your home wasn't just a daily habit; it was supposed to be a pleasure and a hobby. Being efficient and practical, while striving for beauty, became a frequent topic for popular television talk shows like *The Oprah Winfrey Show*.

However, not everyone has Martha Stewart's skills or ingenuity. Thus, professional organizers have become the new "personal trainers" — helping people flex their organizational muscles in their homes.

Downsizing

The more recent trend of companies to downsize, or reduce their number of employees, has created a need for professional organizers. Organizing expert Karen Ussery says that most businesses have seen a decrease in their ability to get and remain organized based on the downsizing of administrative staff. Organizational tasks routinely handled by internal employees are suffering as a result of this trend.

As companies have continued to downsize administrative support staff, the need for organization has increased — creating more and more opportunities for outside consultants. Administrative staff in companies were traditionally those individuals who kept the records, handled the paper, and stored the data — in essence, the organizational staff. With their departure, a door has opened for organizing professionals.

Technology Boom and Data Management

While advances in computer technology have probably increased society's efficiency more than any other single invention in history, it is also true that the use of computers in businesses did not remove the "paper trail." In many cases it allowed people to generate more paper data through efficiency of use.

In other businesses where computers did create less "paperwork," their use increased the need for organization of computer data, a whole new kind of filing and saving that people are relatively unfamiliar with.

Organizing as a Career

Just a few years ago professional organizing as an industry didn't enjoy the reputation and exposure that it does today. "The world is fast becoming aware that professional organization as an industry does exist. It's a new industry and we are building it as we go," says Barry Izsak, president of the National Association of Professional Organizers (NAPO).

He adds that television reality shows about organizing personal space, magazine and news articles about organization, and the awareness brought about by NAPO itself have all added to the dramatic increase in public awareness about this up-and-coming industry. In the last several years NAPO has practically doubled in size annually, and now boasts more than 3,000 members nationwide.

2.2 The Professional Organizer

There are various roles that you will be called upon to fill for clients. You will be amazed at the true breadth and variety of the professional organizing industry. This is truly a profession where you will never get bored. In the sections that follow, you will see who professional organizers are, and the roles they may fill each day.

2.2.1 Characteristics of Pro Organizers

As a professional organizer you will play many roles — each asking you to draw from your personal strengths. Professional organizers seem to share some common personal strengths and interests that help them do their job. Think about if you share any or all of the following traits.

Passionate About Helping People

Professional organizers are a passionate and committed group of people. They are people who care deeply about helping others, and often come to professional organizing from many of the other "helping professions" like teaching or customer service. They all seem to share a deep commitment to their businesses and their clients.

Professional organizers will tell you about what they do with passion and conviction. Organizers come from a helping-mentality and enjoy the process of supporting, facilitating, and nurturing clients. Most professional organizers believe that they are making an impact in their client's lives. They help people to change for the better.

Organized Themselves

Professional organizers are the folks who have "got it together." Organizers lead orderly lives themselves — they are on time for appointments, they have functional home office spaces, and they have filing systems which they have personally designed to work the way they want them to. They have organized contact databases, and they know how to maximize the space they use both for their professional and personal lives.

Communication Pros

Organizers are superb communicators. They can talk to other people and explain ideas and concepts. They have the ability to make people feel better about their organizing dilemmas and positive about potential solutions. They have the ability to coach, to facilitate and to assist. They know how to develop rapport with others. They know how to introduce themselves to a group and explain what they do for a living, and why it is infinitely useful — and fun!

Professional organizers also interact frequently with others in their profession. And since organizers like to communicate, these groups are often lively and interesting exchanges where many feel they make not only professional contacts but also friends.

Business-Minded

Professional organizers are highly motivated businesspeople who are constantly on the lookout for ways that they can distinguish themselves and their businesses and provide something extra.

Professional organizers see everyone they meet as an untapped opportunity. They are naturally friendly and inquisitive about other people's businesses and they look at everyone they meet as someone for their database.

Many professional organizers have created lucrative businesses and most don't see an end to the monetary rewards in sight. They truly feel that this is an industry in which you can build your dream, make as much money and get as much business as you are willing to work for — and organizers work smart, because they know how to maximize their effectiveness.

Responsible and Ethical

Professional organizers are responsible people. Their clients come to them with problems that range from just feeling that they could use some advice about organizational difficulties, to emergency situations that might cost them their jobs (or worse) without organizational intervention. Professional organizers enjoy this responsibility and make sure that their clients walk away from them with solutions and a way to maintain them.

Clients come to rely on organizers for their ability to retain confidential information, and their overall ethical stance. Many professional organizers will tell you that they see vital confidential information on a daily basis in people's homes and in major corporations, and that they pride themselves in creating an atmosphere of ethics and trust.

2.2.2 Are You a "Natural"?

As you will read in this guide, all the skills you need to succeed as a professional organizer can be learned. However, if you are a "born organizer," and have a natural aptitude for organizing, entering this career will be even easier for you.

How do you know if you have what it takes to be a professional organizer? There are several character traits that most professional organizers seem to share. You can test your own aptitude with the quiz on the next page to see if you already have the basic skills you will need, or if you will need to brush up on them before you launch your business.

Many professional organizers share the traits represented by the statements in the quiz. The more questions you answer with either "strongly agree" or "agree," the more qualities you share with working professional organizers.

Self-Evaluation Quiz

Decide how strongly you feel about the following statements, and circle your response on a scale of 1 *(Strongly Disagree)* to 5 *(Strongly Agree)*.

		Strongly Disagree		Neutral		Strongly Agree
1.	I am motivated by helping others.	1	2	3	4	5
2.	I enjoy achieving goals.	1	2	3	4	5
3.	I like structure.	1	2	3	4	5
4.	I am a good listener.	1	2	3	4	5
5.	I enjoy interacting with others.	1	2	3	4	5
6.	I feel comfortable in one-on-one situations.	1	2	3	4	5
7.	I have been told I have good taste.	1	2	3	4	5
8.	I look for solutions.	1	2	3	4	5
9.	I am a positive person.	1	2	3	4	5
10.	I prefer to adhere to a schedule.	1	2	3	4	5
11.	I can break projects down into doable tasks.	1	2	3	4	5
12.	I am not easily overwhelmed.	1	2	3	4	5
13.	I am not critical or judgmental.	1	2	3	4	5
14.	I am empathetic.	1	2	3	4	5
15.	I am imaginative.	1	2	3	4	5
16.	I like order.	1	2	3	4	5
17.	I am energetic.	1	2	3	4	5
18.	I can often see more than one solution to a problem.	1	2	3	4	5
19.	I am responsive to the needs of others.	1	2	3	4	5

Note that a neutral answer, or one in which you disagree or strongly disagree, is not an indication that you should not be a professional organizer. It may instead indicate areas you do not consider your strong points, and you may need additional training or experience. You may also choose not to make those aspects of the business your focus. For example, if you have less energy, you might not take on garage organization.

Take a good look at your skills. What do you know how to do really well? What are you qualified to advise people about? What do you consider yourself an expert in? Like most professional organizers, you will have some skill areas in which you consider yourself a specialist, and others that you are less knowledgeable and proficient in.

Take some time and make a list. Decide which areas of professional organizing are your greatest strengths. Once you start to actually write down your skill strengths you will probably be pleasantly surprised to find that you have more than you imagined. This beginning list will prove useful later as you determine the list of services your business will offer.

2.2.3 The Roles You Will Play

As mentioned, your "role" as a professional organizer can take on a variety of forms, depending on the situation and what the client needs. Be prepared to be needed not only for your ability to organize, but for your talents in the following areas of expertise.

General Roles

Consultant

> *"When I work with someone, my approach is based on… their way of thinking, their style, and their needs."*
>
> — Karen Ussery, Professional Organizer

A professional organizer is expected to provide consulting services to their clients. As a consultant you will need to be able to:

- Determine the needs of your client through interviewing and fact-finding sessions

- Diagnose the problem areas or concerns

- Decide how your skills can assist those needs

- Formulate a program or plan to assist your client

- Present your plan to the client

- Estimate the length and cost of the job

- Communicate effectively with the client and reach agreement about the plan

- Work with the client to implement the plan

- Provide the client with necessary tools and resources to continue the program or plan you devise

Counselor

"It's important to be nonjudgmental… [Just] because someone needs to get organized, it doesn't make him or her a bad person."

— Barry Izsak, Professional Organizer

While professional organizers usually aren't trained therapists, they are in a unique position in which they have access to the most personal elements of their clients' lives and histories. Professional organizers often become a trusted advisor to clients, in much the same way people trust their doctors or clergy members with confidential information.

This unique position requires a level of personal accountability. As a professional organizer, you must determine your own code of ethics and stick to it in order to ensure that clients can feel comfortable not only letting you into their homes and offices, but also often deeply into their lives.

The NAPO has a published code of ethics for its members, which you can read at **www.napo.net/get_organized/ethics.html**.

The C.A.R.E. Concept

Sometimes using an acronym is an easy way to remember information or to quickly develop a mental link to a concept. Think about the acronym C.A.R.E. to help you remember the unique responsibilities of being a counselor to your clients:

Compassion and Concern
Active Listening and Attention
Responsibility and Respect
Empathy and Encouragement

Compassion and Concern

When new clients bring you into their homes or offices and show you the clutter, the problems, the personal papers and the archives from their past, they are showing you the most intimate details of their lives. The reason that most clients will call you in the first place is that they find themselves in unmanageable situations. That trust makes you responsible for protecting them and treating them with compassion and concern.

It is vital that you come into each client situation with a non-judgmental attitude. Whatever situation clients find themselves in, they are already feeling the negative emotions that result from not being able to make the situation work. Before you open your briefcase and take out a pen, you will want to first establish trust with a friendly sense of caring and a nonjudgmental attitude toward their situation.

Active Listening and Attention

To be able to determine the cure for your client's situation, you must first understand the problem. Even if you are the most experienced professional organizer in the world and feel you have seen it all, all clients' lives and situations are unique, and each deserves your total attention. Listening may be the most vital thing you do all day to ensure your professional success in this business.

Empathy and Encouragement

Empathy, or attempted understanding of your clients' situations, will help them to feel hopeful about change. Encouragement will let them feel like they can improve their situation and feel positive about the future. Make sure you showcase both of these to potential and existing clients.

Responsibility and Respect

When clients share their problems with you they share all kinds of personal information, from family issues to credit card numbers and tax information. You must go into the situation with a great understanding of the personal responsibility you have to respect clients' confidentiality and privacy. Clients will trust you with everything, and you have to pledge to them (and to yourself) to protect their information. Many organizers use a written pledge of confidentiality to drive this point home.

Teacher

"I tell my clients that with organizing you have to develop new skills. It is just like trying to learn a sport. You have to take lessons, and then you have to practice."

— Chris McKenry, Professional Organizer

You may not think of yourself as a teacher, but as a professional organizer you are someone who develops a lesson to teach, thinks about how to teach that lesson, models it for their "student" (in this case your clients), and then makes sure that clients can master particular lessons and learn the skills.

It is important to teach clients how to do things for themselves, because otherwise the best laid plans for organization only work for as long as the professional organizer is standing there. It's like the concept of teaching someone to fish rather than providing that person with a fish — one lasts forever, one makes a nice meal. The goal of a professional organizer is to teach clients to fish — that is, to be able to organize themselves.

Good teachers are able to break down a task into a series of parts. For each "subject" you teach as a professional organizer, you will take the time to look closely at your own methods and determine the steps. Then you will need to determine how to best model the steps and explain the directions and relevance of each step. Unlike in a school, teaching adult clients who are paying for your services requires that you let them know why a skill is important to learn and what the benefits of learning it are — or, what's in it for them!

Finally, as you teach your clients how to organize themselves, it's helpful to develop tools such as systems, worksheets or surveys, lists, and forms that they can take away and review again as needed. You will find a number of these throughout this guide for you to use.

Specific Organizing Roles

Home Economist

"I have a degree in family studies, so I am very interested in how families work, how the systems work, and how the individuals in the family affect the system."

— Laurene Livesey Park, Professional Organizer

Your knowledge of how to run a home efficiently, and how to keep it organized and running smoothly for all the people who live there, is another important skill. All homes must be run in a manner that makes it possible for people to go about their daily routine.

If you offer home organization services, you will go into clients' homes and show them how to make their homes "work." While you will want to make it clear to clients that you are not a cleaning service or a substitute mother, you may step in and do hands-on rearranging for clients.

You may be called upon to make any of the following home living spaces work efficiently:

- Kitchens

- Laundry rooms

- Home offices

- Children's rooms or play areas

- Living rooms

- Dining rooms

- Basements and attics

- Garages

- Craft rooms or workrooms

- Storage areas

- Closets and cupboards

When you work with people in their homes you will need to have an understanding of what they want to accomplish in the space, what routines and tasks they do every day, and how they want things to work. Your goal as a home economist is to help people make their homes a well-ordered and efficient space that fits with their own definition of a happy home.

Information Systems Expert

"I work with clients sitting with them at their computer so that everything they are doing is at their machine, they are hands on, and they are doing the tasks."

— Rozanne Hird, Professional Organizer

Whether you deal with novices who want to computerize their address books, or clients at corporations who have a complex network of computers running a variety of software, having technological experience and ability is a definite plus for a professional organizer. This doesn't mean that you will need to be a programmer, but that you can help clients:

- Set up file and information retrieval systems

- Create databases

- Maintain schedules and calendars

- Use goal and time management programs

The wide variety of amazing organizational software available today makes a personal computer one of the best tools that a professional organizer can use – and teach clients to use – effectively. There is software for every organizational need that clients might have, whether they are trying to organize their monthly bills at home or their entire department at work.

Like anything else, computer skills are learned and increase with time. Some professional organizers make computer organizational services a large part of their services, others do not. However, if you are going to provide services for businesses – from home offices to corporations – you will find that computer savvy is a must.

Knowledge Management Expert

"I work with clients a maximum of two hours at a time because… after the first couple of hours, people don't remember anything."

— Rozanne Hird, Professional Organizer

Knowledge management is an important-sounding term for things we do every day. It is the ability to record and classify, then retrieve and reuse knowledge.

You will help clients decide what knowledge they should retain permanently, what form it should take, and how they will retrieve it and use it again later on. You will help clients look at their homes and offices and classify and organize what they find there.

For example, in clients' homes you might help them classify and organize for retrieval and reuse the following sort of things:

- Personal records

- Bills

- Personal libraries

- Memorabilia

- Family scrapbooks and photo albums

- Home movies and slides

- Genealogy research

In business places you might help clients classify and organize for retrieval and reuse the following sort of things:

- Procedures

- Instructions

- Policies

- Protocol

- Intellectual property

- Proprietary information or trade secrets

- Operations manuals

- Company history

- Company libraries

Office Manager

"I… go in and assess their administrative systems and processes and procedures to see where they can be streamlined, and how I can help them improve the flow of information so that people are working more efficiently."

— Carol Halsey, Professional Organizer

People need to have their professional lives organized. In fact, many clients feel that the organizational systems in their workspaces are the most vital aspects of their organization, and the ones they need to address first. Some of the ways you might be asked to help clients organize their offices or workspaces include:

- Creating and maintaining filing systems

- Organizing online or computerized databases

- Creating workflow systems

- Creating computerized address books and contact retrieval systems

- Schedule and calendar organization

- Time management

- Goal-setting

It helps to be familiar with how offices work in general. Many organizers come to professional organizing from careers in business. This experience gives them practical, hands-on experience in office environments, and an understanding of how offices work.

Think about office-related work you have done. Have you organized your own filing system? Did you keep books or records? Did you use a computer to organize your calendar or appointments? Thinking about what you have done personally will help you to transfer your applicable skills and harness those you can package into a service you can sell to clients.

Even if you have not spent much time working in office environments, if you are proficient at organizing and good at listening to the needs of your clients you will be able to develop office systems that work. Any system you have created for your own life is something you can draw on as a professional organizer. You may also decide to train in a specific software program or to take a class to help you hone your skills.

Space Designer

"Too often we just consider how to decorate a space without applying the function that is required. Sleek, smooth surfaces may be stylish, but have the storage needs been considered in every room of the house?"

— Chris McKenry, Professional Organizer

Just like professionals in the interior design industry, organizers must be able to see a space and figure out how to transform it into a functional living or working space. And it isn't enough to just make it "functional"; clients also want beautiful surroundings in which to live and work.

This isn't to say that all professional organizers are interior decorators — however, some of them definitely do have highly developed decorating skills. In some cases you may work in tandem with decorators, builders, and carpenters to help clients achieve exactly the look they want for their spaces, as well as the designs that will provide clients with the most organizational utility.

Professional organizers stay up to date on design trends that are in vogue at any given time. For example, many professional organizers help clients establish living and working spaces based on the principles of Feng Shui — an Eastern design philosophy in which order and peace are achieved through harmonic placement of objects in a room.

Professional organizers realize that they must be sensitive to the style needs of their clients. They make organizational tools fit an overall theme or design choice in a home or office.

Time Management Coach

"There is no 'one right way' to organize... Because people think and process information differently, your system has to be a reflection of the way they organize information in their minds. Your environment is organized when it's a reflection of your brain."

— Karen Ussery, Professional Organizer

Many of your clients will be overscheduled and overcommitted — not only at work, but also in their communities, at school, at church, and even at home. Time management, and the resulting ability to schedule short- and long-term goals, is a skill you can teach to your clients.

Often clients will tell you that they don't have the time to get organized! People who are in the throes of clutter and disorganization have lost their ability to control or use their time wisely — even though some don't know it, their disorganization is contributing to their inability to manage time. It's all related.

While most professional organizers work with clients showing them how to control their physical space, others choose to teach time management and goal-setting skills, too. As a time management coach you might help clients:

- Evaluate their "time drains"

- Create daily schedules

- Determine their short- and long-term goals

- Streamline their activities at home or in the office

- Plan for special events

Time management and goal setting methodology and techniques will help clients plan for their dreams and have enough time to go after them. Section 3.3 has more information on the tools and techniques you will use to teach these skills.

Other Roles

Customer Service Specialist

"My clients tell me I become like a daughter to them in some ways. It doesn't matter when they call me, I would rather they call me than to worry about anything. I wear a cell phone. I am not a 9-to-5 person. And I let my clients contact me any time."

— Brenda Clements, Professional Organizer

Think about the people in your life that you buy services from. Think about the doctors you have liked and respected, the teacher you feel really made a difference, even the plumbers or the car repair people you like and trust. Why do you like them?

Well, partly because they are good at what they do. But also, and just as important, they treat you with respect, they listen to your questions and problems and they hear what you need and respond to it. There is far more to being a professional organizer than just the ability to organize. You, like these other people in service or helping professions, need to be a customer service expert.

Customer service is the art of making customers feel validated. Clients are looking for things that they may not tell you, or even know on a conscious level:

- Honesty

- Integrity

- Goodwill

- Respect

- Courtesy

People with excellent customer service skills have the ability to hear what their clients are saying, what they want, and what they need. They have excellent listening skills, and they have the ability to put themselves in the place of their clients.

Friend

"While you should remain professional with clients, at the same time you want to be friendly. There is a fine line that you have to walk in order to maintain the client/professional organizer relationship…"

— Chris McKenry, Professional Organizer

Being friendly with your clients – someone who they enjoy having in their homes and offices – is one of the most important things you can do to establish good working relationships. Friendliness and a positive attitude put clients at ease in a potentially awkward situation, and help you to build the rapport you need to get the job done.

Many professional organizers feel they truly become part of their clients' support systems, but it's important to learn to blend a friendly attitude and a supportive demeanor with the right degree of professionalism and detachment. That blend becomes finely tuned with time on the job. Let the clients set the tone, and treat them the way you would appreciate if you were in their shoes.

Friendliness also affects your bottom line. Clients who enjoy working with you will feel confident enough to mention you to colleagues, to family members, and to friends. It is a well-known tenet of business that clients prefer to do business with people that they genuinely like as people.

Networking Professional

"I get… referrals from existing clients, clients who are referrals from friends, business associates, people who have met me at various organizations — so it is a lot more 'controlled' than just putting an ad in a local paper."

— Rozanne Hird, Professional Organizer

You probably know people who are natural networkers. They always seem to be spreading interesting and relevant information. They know just the right business to send you to so you get what you need, and they aren't afraid to talk about what they do and how they can help someone. You too can become this type of person, if you aren't already.

Professional organizers cite their networking skills as most important to develop and grow their businesses. Networking is the art of connecting effectively in your community with those who can help you. It allows you to interact with people who can give you advice, lead you to clients, and who can serve as referral sources.

Networking is something that you can begin today. Just think of everyone you know – both personally and professionally – and you have the beginnings of a business network. Everyone you come into contact with is potentially someone who can help you, or someone you can help. That's how networking works — it's the world's best, no-cost service that everyone can share and profit from.

You can network anywhere and with anyone, from chatting on your phone while wearing your bathrobe and sipping coffee, to joining any of the many networking organizations and business groups in your community. Section 5.2.1 will teach you more about honing this desirable skill for professional organizers.

Public Speaker

"Speaking is part of my business. [Before one presentation] I had locked my keys in my car and I was relating the story. I was telling the story and laughing about it as part of my presentation. I said, 'Hey, I am disorganized too. Sometimes it's still a struggle for me.' And three people leaned over and picked up my business card!"

— Laurene Livesey Park, Professional Organizer

Professional organizers are excellent communicators, and with that ability often comes the opportunity to act as a public speaker. In fact, many professional organizers routinely use opportunities to speak in public as a way to promote their businesses.

Being able to stand up in front of a group and talk to people about your ideas on organizing is something that comes naturally for many organizers. Really it is just doing what you do every day – instructing and coaching about organization – for a larger audience. Even if you have never presented in front of a group, it is something you can learn to do with time, practice, and the tips you'll read later in this guide.

When you teach, coach, and answer questions for clients, you are laying the groundwork for your public speaking career. Make a note of how you communicate ideas, the steps you use to explain a process, and how you answer the questions your clients ask. Soon you will have the beginnings of a wonderful presentation.

2.2.4 Ways to Specialize

Each professional organizer can create a business that best represents his or her strengths and passions. While there are certainly traits you will share with other organizers – the ability to create order out of chaos, time management skills, an affinity for creating workable plans and systems, office organization skills and home management skills – your specialty, or the things that you do best, can be as unique as you can imagine.

While some professional organizers consider themselves generalists – those who are willing to take on practically any challenge, no matter what – others consider themselves specialists and have (or acquire) special talents and professional backgrounds to create a definite focus to their businesses. Specialists help clients with specific needs. Read on to see some of the various specialties you can decide to focus on as a professional organizer.

Residential

Residential specialists help people with the everyday challenges of creating an organized home. They help clients make their living spaces livable. They organize kitchens, closets, garages, etc., or focus on one or two areas. For example, some professional organizers absolutely love and excel at closet organization and have built whole businesses out of just doing that, while others focus on kitchens.

Home Office/Small Office

Home office/small office specialists know how to help their clients organize their space to best enable them to run their own successful small businesses, or telecommute effectively from home. They help clients set up filing systems, databases or other information management systems. Many professional organizers who gravitate toward this specialty come from office support, secretarial, or administrative backgrounds.

Corporate

If you have ever worked for a large corporation you know that things are done quite differently than they are in a small company. There are a variety of rules and procedures to consider. Even moving a filing cabinet can require filling out a variety of forms.

Corporate specialists enjoy working in large business environments, and understand the policies, procedures, and bureaucracy of the corporate structure. Organizational challenges on a corporate level can range from organizing individual workspaces, to analyzing workflow processes or project management. Most corporate specialists come from a corporate background.

In many cases you will be required to bid for corporate jobs, write a proposal, and invoice the company for your services. Corporate specialists sometimes work with specific individuals inside a company, while other times they are hired to assist a whole department full of people with their organizational challenges.

Training

A professional organizer who focuses on training will teach groups about how to get organized, based on a specific curriculum that they have developed. Some trainers teach through junior or community colleges, others work with corporations, and still others are personal coaches who offer one-on-one guidance to individuals.

Professional organizers who develop this specialty are often those who write books or articles, are quoted for newspapers, and sometimes even appear on television, since they are already talented and personable communicators.

Speaking

Professional organizers who specialize in speaking publicly often find themselves employed not only as organizers, but also as full-time professional speakers.

They might begin their career by using free speaking engagements as a way to attract business, but find they spend less and less time in one-on-one appointments and more time being paid to speak to large groups about organization topics. This is a potentially lucrative specialization once you are comfortable with public speaking.

Financial

Let's face it — there are some people who know more about the world of finance and accounting than most. Financial organizers have a unique blend of knowing numbers and knowing people, too. This is a desirable combination, as not all "numbers people" are clear and personable communicators.

Specializing in this area requires that a professional organizer has a background in finance or accounting. Many times these professional organizers come from careers in corporations and find that their expertise makes them perfect consultants in this area.

Technical

So much of how people organize their lives today has something to do with technical equipment of some kind. Many clients need professional organizers to help them make all these pieces of technology work together. We all know what it's like to have an email inbox that is overflowing with messages that need a response, and no system to organize them. Thus, the technical specialist was born.

Technical specialists help clients organize anything from computer files, databases, address books, contact software and email, to personal digital assistants (PDAs) and smart phones.

Families

Family specialists deal with the challenges that families have in getting and staying organized. They might help parents figure out ways to streamline their morning routine, or help children set up effective homework spaces and strategies.

They can help the person in the family who takes on the major role in organizing and delegating responsibility establish ways to get others in the family involved in organizing systems and routines.

Organizers with this specialty often are parents who have organized their own family effectively, or those who have experience as teachers, psychologists, or social workers. Quite often a family specialist is also a residential specialist.

Seniors

Seniors moving from larger homes into smaller ones, or perhaps into assisted living situations, need professional organizers to help them go through a lifetime of possessions, and to figure out what is practical for their new space and situation.

Specializing with seniors requires that professional organizers have an affinity for working with older people and sensitivity toward what sometimes are very difficult transitions. Professional organizers who specialize in working with seniors report that the experience is very rewarding, and that they feel appreciated by their clients.

ADD/ADHD

Both Attention Deficit Disorder (ADD) and Attention Deficit/Hyperactivity Disorder (ADHD) are medical conditions that affect sufferers with the inability to focus on tasks. Some professional organizers choose to specifically help people with ADD and ADHD with their organizational dilemmas.

These specialists need to have an understanding of the medical conditions and their impact on organization, which is often gained through personal experience with family members or friends.

Feng Shui

Feng Shui (pronounced *fung schway*) is the Chinese art of creating harmonious surroundings in order to balance one's Chi (pronounced *chee*), or life energy. This technique allows people to see and deal with their disorganization on a variety of levels, including the emotional and the spiritual. Feng Shui experts say that this art and philosophy helps people create balanced lives at both home and work.

Many professional organizers have gravitated to Feng Shui, not only because there are scores of clients who are interested in it, but also because, for many, it makes sense. You can add Feng Shui to your list of skills, and apply it in any organizational situation, or make it a true specialty on its own.

Relocation (Moving)

One thing never changes — people sell their houses, and need to decide what goes and what stays. For people with a lot of "stuff" or those who have been at one location for many years, relocating sometimes requires expert assistance.

Relocation specialists help clients sort through mountains of belongings, making decisions about what stays and what goes, and packing belongings in an organized fashion so that they arrive at the new home site in order.

Some professional organizers who work in this specialty area coordinate with other professional organizers at their clients' destination points and work in tandem to ensure moves go off as planned.

Emergency Services

There are some people who have gotten to a point where their clutter has become not only a personal nuisance, but a crisis. This dilemma is the specialty of professional organizers who provide emergency services.

Professional organizers who specialize in this area report that sometimes they are called to help people who have had a catastrophic illness in the family or to help someone who is elderly. This specialty requires an exceptional type of personal organizer with tact, sensitivity and a nonjudgmental attitude, as you may find yourself working with social workers, law enforcement or other local government employees, and comforting distraught family members.

Create Your Own Specialty

As you can see, there are a variety of identified specialties in the professional organizing industry — with more being developed daily. One interesting thing about this industry is that it is defined by the creativity and imagination of the people in it. You may find that you create a new specialty as you develop your own professional organizing business.

3. How to Organize

*"My business started when I made a New Year's resolution about five or
six years ago to get myself organized. Out of that came the realization
that, 'Gee, if I can teach myself to do it, then I can teach other people to
do it!'"*

— Laurene Livesey Park, Organize Me 101

There you have it from a successful professional... everyone started
somewhere. And while many people preparing for a career in the professional organizing industry consider themselves completely organized,
you may not fully understand the systems you already use.

In this chapter you will review basic organizing principles, and then apply
them to different areas of human life, including personal organization,
home organization, and business organization.

Remember that it isn't enough just to be organized; you have to be able to think through the way you organize yourself, and why it works. This is the essence of professional organizing — being able to think about, describe, and implement the systems of organization you use in your own life, and teach them to your clients.

By the time you get to the end of the chapter, you will have a thorough understanding of the principles of organization and a "toolbox" of techniques you can begin to use with your very first client.

3.1 Organizing Systems

In this first section, we'll take a look at what makes a person organized. How does it happen that some people are organized and some not? Are you a natural organizer or a conscious organizer?

Organizers base almost all of what they do on their ability to create workable and orderly systems. But have you ever stopped to consider the parts of a system and how to create one? This section reveals the basics of creating an organized system — everything it takes to create the parts of any system for anything, step by step.

3.1.1 What Makes a Person "Organized"?

"Getting organized is not an inherited trait; it's a learned behavior."

— Barry Izsak, Professional Organizer

There are many characteristics and attitudes that organized people share. For example, you might:

- Enjoy order

- Feel serene in uncomplicated surroundings

- Consider yourself calm

- Be self-motivated and disciplined

- Always be thinking of a better way to do something

- Have a neat and orderly home

- Like to be in control

- Be trustworthy and serious about keeping your commitments

- Keep a personal schedule of activities

- Invent things and find solutions easily

- Enjoy structure, including rules, systems, and procedures

- Make deliberate choices

In addition to possessing some or many of these characteristics, organizers generally fall into one of two categories: the naturally organized or the consciously organized. You can also be a little of both.

Some people say they crawled out of their cradle organized. Some even say they have "organized genes." While it may be true that certain personality types gravitate to the industry, to be truly organized you have to be cognizant of it, too — especially if you are going to teach someone else to do it.

A natural organizer could be thought of as a naturally gifted artist. They might be able to paint a masterpiece, but may not be aware of how they do it. An art teacher, however, must master his craft. He must know why he uses one brush or another; he must select the proper tools, and know how to use them to get the results he wants. If you are naturally organized and want to teach others to get organized, you may need to take some time to analyze your systems… this chapter will help you do just that.

A conscious organizer is someone who has gone through the process of organization and thought through how she does it. She has purposely considered the steps she takes to do something, how she does it, and why. She is often self-taught — having moved from less than organized to organized through her own planning, development, and implementation.

3.1.2 Creating a Basic System

"[Organizing is] not a 'one-size fits all' solution. The important thing is that the system works for the client, that a client likes the system, and is able to maintain it. You have to take into account the way… each individual works."

— Barry Izsak, Professional Organizer

Most professional organizers have a system of organizing. They have figured out a way to do things, and after a while, if they are successful, they have figured out a way to apply their system to other people's lives. They have fine-tuned it and refined it long enough to know what works and what doesn't. Many organizational systems are based on 10 common steps, explained below.

The 10 Steps of a Successful System

1. Assessing the Situation or Problem

As you begin to look over any organizational scenario, you need to take an overview. The best place to start is a general one — you need to get an overall impression of the current situation and how successfully organized you consider it to be.

2. Determining a Desirable Outcome

Before you begin to organize an area, envision the best possible outcome as you see it today. Visualizing the best-case scenario will give you a starting place to determine what needs to be done to get from where it is today to where you ultimately want to see it.

3. Identifying What Works

Identify the system in place and what is currently working. You have undoubtedly heard the expression, "If it isn't broken, don't fix it." Take a look at what is currently working and identify why it works.

4. Identifying What is NOT Working

As you begin to notice what works you will also have other, somewhat more glaring information, about what does not work. Sometimes this will be practically everything — or sometimes it can be just a few things.

Usually the things that don't work in an organizational system are those things that are really annoying and waste time and energy.

5. Outlining a Plan

To get something organized you have to develop a plan. To begin with, what sort of knowledge or expertise will you need to complete this organizational task? Is this knowledge you already have, or will you have to learn something first? For example, if you are adding information to a new PDA, first you might need to become familiar with the way it works.

6. Determining the Action Steps in the Plan

How will you get from the problem to the solution? What steps will you need to take? Where exactly do you start? How complicated will it be? What tools will you need? Is there anything that will have to happen before you can begin? Sit down and map out the steps you will take to achieve a desired organizational result.

7. Implementing the Plan

This is the execution stage of the process, where you roll up your sleeves and do whatever it is that needs to be done to create order. This will undoubtedly be done in steps according to how you have laid out your plan or your implementation procedures. In this phase of organization you will take action one step at a time and recognize the small accomplishments along the way to your major organizational goal.

8. Altering the Plan

As you implement any organizational plan you will see things you need to "tweak" or correct as you go along. Being able to slightly alter your course to correct something will save you a world of time. Just because you have a plan doesn't mean you can't alter it slightly.

9. Assessing the Outcome

Assessment is a vital tool. It allows you to test your organizational system, get feedback, and find out how it works. This is the stage where you can see how much you like a new system and determine the "bugs," so to speak. Don't expect perfection, but expect competent, workable results. This is success. It's a learning process.

10. Refining and Improving

Sometimes it takes a while to refine a new system. It has to be put to the test under normal, everyday conditions to see if it works. This is why you need to have time to have a new system in place, see it work, assess it, and then decide how to refine it to work the way you want, as many times as is needed.

Do You Already Have a System?

Without knowing it, you probably do have a problem-solving system, based on the ten steps of a successful system listed above. Think about what you do when you walk into a messy bathroom...

> You take a look around the bathroom and decide it's time to clean, knowing it will make the bathroom more usable. Thankfully the cleaning product you put in the toilet that dispenses with each flush makes that an easy job, but as you scrape soap off the soap dish, you realize a hand pump would save you this task. You make a mental note to buy one, and resolve to do that tomorrow.
>
> When you put the pump in place the next day, you realize it doesn't hold much soap, so you'll have to buy a larger refill container to keep on hand. But the new pump looks great, and there is no more soap dish to clean. Your husband/wife walks into the bathroom to wash up, and looks around blankly. "Where's the soap dish my mother gave me?" he/she asks. Well, maybe the soap dish has to come back out, but will be used for decorative soaps only...

Even in this brief example, you have gone through the ten steps of a successful organizing system! While you may have your own way of getting things done, your system should include at least those ten steps in order to be complete and thorough.

3.2 Five Key Organizing Principles

Organizers are constantly trying to package the concepts and principles of organization in fun, useful, and easy ways for their clients to remember. In this section you will get a variety of handy teaching tools –

concepts and principles – packaged and ready to use with your clients immediately. These tools will help you communicate with clients, teach them, and help them move to the next level in their own organization as easy as one, two, three! They are described here as:

- Minimize, Maximize, and Maintain

- Condition and Calamity

- Objective, Tools, and Steps (OTS)

- Treasure, Trash, Tools, or Toys

- C.O.P.E. — Category, Order, Proximity, and Ease of Use

3.2.1 Minimize, Maximize, and Maintain

You will teach your clients to minimize clutter, maximize space, and maintain the order these actions create.

Minimize

Probably one of the most important concepts in organization is the idea that, to be organized, you must minimize belongings, stuff, or things in any space. Professional organizers all talk about purging, tossing, recycling, removing, discarding, donating, and throwing away. One of the primary reasons clients find themselves disorganized is that they have not learned, or taken to heart, the principal of minimization.

To be organized you must minimize.

Maximize

Clients must learn to maximize the way they use space and take the best advantage of the space available. You will help them check to see that it isn't misused in a way that is inefficient. This also applies to the tools and the "stuff" in the space. Everything must be maximized — that is, used to its best advantage.

To be organized you must maximize.

MMM Form

Room or Area: _____

How can I minimize?

1. _____
2. _____
3. _____
4. _____
5. _____

How can I maximize?

1. _____
2. _____
3. _____
4. _____
5. _____

How can I maintain?

1. _____
2. _____
3. _____
4. _____
5. _____

Maintain

The third concept in this trio is maintaining order. For clients to be organized they must constantly maintain the other two concepts described above — they must constantly minimize what they have around them, throwing things away, removing them or recycling them, and they must constantly maximize the effective use of their surroundings. Order is a constant process. It is fluid and changeable, simply because organized spaces are used and altered daily.

To be organized you must maintain.

MMM Form

On the facing page is a sample *MMM Form* which you can use to apply the MMM concept for each room or area you wish to organize. (The form is also included on the CD-ROM attached to the inside back cover of this book.) Make notes and brainstorm solutions with the client for each area. Use the notes you take to help you formulate your organizational plan.

3.2.2 Condition and Calamity

"What a calamity!" In the case of organization, a calamity is the worst sort of misfortune, mishap, or disastrous result that happens because an area of organization is out of control. The condition is the current state of organization in a given area.

For example, imagine the following condition: the client's bills for the last six months are mixed up and tossed in a heap on the table, so that they don't know where anything is. A calamitous result could be that they miss their mortgage payment, or have their electricity shut off. It's easy to see there are times when disorganization can produce a calamity.

Understanding the condition an organizational area is in and realizing the level of potential calamity that will result if it is left unresolved is the concept of Condition and Calamity, which you can use to help prioritize tasks.

Using C&C to Prioritize

It will be easy for you to see areas of clients' lives that need to be organized; however, clients will have to tell you how important they are.

Being able to judge the importance and relevance of organizational tasks is one of the major principles of organization. To decide what level of importance to place on an organizational area of life, you must be able to determine the potential resulting problems if left unresolved. That is:

What is going to happen if this doesn't get organized?

Sometimes the answer will be: nothing. And sometimes the answer will be — a calamity! This will allow you to help them see what should be done first, second, third, and so on.

Your first order of business will be the areas in the worst condition, with the worst possible calamity. Sometimes an organizational area can be in terrible shape, but the potential calamity is relatively minor. You can consider leaving these areas for a later time, and focusing on the biggest concerns.

A sample *Condition and Calamity Form* appears on the facing page and is included on the CD-ROM that comes with this book.

3.2.3 Treasure, Trash, Tools, or Toys

One of the most important principles of organization is the concept of assigned worth. Being able to determine the relative worth of things allows us to make decisions about them. What are these "things" clients have in their lives – all their stuff – and what are they for? What is their value to clients? Sometimes even the client will have a hard time deciding.

A professional organizer must assist and teach clients to assign value to things they own so clients can make their own decisions about what is valuable to them. You can help your clients categorize their possessions by examining each item's value in terms of function and emotion.

Condition and Calamity Form

List each organizational area and the condition it is currently in: **P**oor, **F**air, **G**ood, or **E**xcellent. Then, determine what the potential calamity is if the area is not organized immediately.

Area: **Condition:**   **Calamity:**

1. _____   P   F   G   E   _____

   _____   _____

2. _____   P   F   G   E   _____

   _____   _____

3. _____   P   F   G   E   _____

   _____   _____

4. _____   P   F   G   E   _____

   _____   _____

5. _____   P   F   G   E   _____

   _____   _____

6. _____   P   F   G   E   _____

   _____   _____

7. _____   P   F   G   E   _____

   _____   _____

Functional and Emotional Value

To determine the functional value of an item, ask the client how useful and essential the item is in their life. This can be determined by examining how often the item is used (if at all). A vacuum cleaner has a high function value to someone with wall-to-wall carpeting. However, it has a low function value to someone who had carpeting in their last house, but then moved into a place with beautiful hardwood and is holding onto it "just in case."

You will also hear items described as having "personal value" or "sentimental value." These are things we own because of an emotional attachment to it. A lock of someone's hair is an example of a thing owned purely for emotional reasons. A picture, a letter, a photograph, an art object made by a child — these are all examples of things that are owned for emotional reasons, but that have little or no functional value.

The Four Categories of Possessions

Once you understand the concepts of function and emotion, you will see that all things that people own fall into four categories:

- *Treasure* (high emotion, low function)

- *Trash* (low emotion, low function)

- *Tools* (low emotion, high function)

- *Toys* (high emotion, high function)

Treasure

A treasure is something that is highly emotional, but not highly functional. Its value is the emotion it represents. An antique doll passed down from generation to generation in a family may or may not have a lot of monetary value, but it may be beautiful or ornamental, it may have personal history attached to it, and it is something that the owner feels a high level of emotion about.

Trash

Suppose clients have belongings that have no function and also no emotional value. This is what we lovingly call trash.

Think of things that are broken, that don't do what they are supposed to do, or that clients never really liked. Think of things that are out of date, or that have been replaced by something clients like better. If clients don't like it (emotion) and they don't use it (function) it is trash, and trash is what professional organizers love to purge.

Tools

A tool has a function, but little or no emotional value. It is usable; it serves a purpose. It can be a lawn mower or a safety pin — the only requirement is that it has a function, and that the owner of the tool uses the tool. Tools are the belongings people have that make their lives function properly.

Toys

Now, let's say clients own things that are functional and emotional to them. If a man working happily in his garage feels emotional about his tools, they are actually toys.

A toy, by distinction, is something clients can use that they also have emotion about — usually happiness or excitement. An example might be a computer or TV — it is extremely useful, as well as something the client is really attached to.

Using "The 4 Ts" to Organize

Once you can categorize your client's items into treasure, trash, tools, or toys, it will be easier to see what should be done to organize these items. Go through any area you are ready to organize and see where the items you are trying to decide about fall. Then you will be ready to identify what is important and why, and what stays and what goes.

Tools	Put tools in a convenient place where they can find them again to use.

Treasures   Put their treasures somewhere where they are beautifully displayed or safety stored. You need to help them decide how many treasures are too many for any given space. When you are helping a client decide about whether to display or store, ask them if the item is active or passive. Active are things they love to look at, display, and have around them every day. Passive are things that are important to them but they may choose to store. For example, clients might choose to display their dolls but decide that their family genealogy materials need to be stored.

Toys   Put toys in places where they are ready to use and can be easily enjoyed. Nothing is as frustrating as having "cool stuff" that isn't conveniently placed or ready to go.

Trash   Remind clients that trash is the stuff they don't use and don't like. Help clients let go of their trash. First they have to see it for what it is, and then they have to transfer it some way — a trash can, or a recycling bin. Many people feel more comfortable giving useable things away rather than throwing them away. There are hundreds of places that truly need clients' "trash" or transferable items. If there are large items to get rid of, you can suggest a refuse pick up service like 1-800-Got-Junk (**www.1800gotjunk.com**).

TIP: You will want to be sensitive to your clients' concepts of what is important to them personally. A professional organizer can give clients insight and advice about what to do with their "stuff," but the final decision about which things have value in clients' lives is their responsibility. You can only teach and facilitate — you can't decide for them.

"The 4 Ts" Grid for Clients

Use the grid below to organize belongings into four areas. You can do this mentally, or write them into one of the boxes shown. Remember:

- *Treasure* (high emotion, low function)

- *Trash* (low emotion, low function)

- *Tools* (low emotion, high function)

- *Toys* (high emotion, high function)

4 Ts Grid

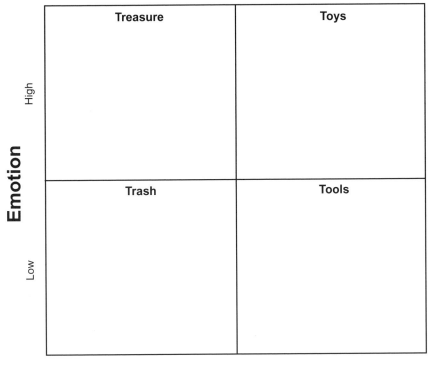

3.2.4 Objective, Tools, and Steps

It is possible to understand the idea of order, to understand the concepts, and still live in disorder. You will have clients who definitely understand the concepts of organization but for some reason are still swimming in stuff. This is often because they haven't learned to take the action steps.

This doesn't mean that deciding what to do isn't important — it is. Clients who act without thinking are as disorganized as those who think and don't act. However, taking action after they decide what to do is the step that changes chaos into order. Without this step, it is all talk. The action step requires that you help clients take what they have learned about their disorganization problem and make a plan. This plan includes the following:

The Objective

The reason or the goal for a plan. For example, "Getting last year's bills organized and filed."

The Tools

Tools, in this case, by definition, are the things needed to organize the stuff. They can be anything from a filing cabinet to a modular closet system, to a basket.

The Steps

Planning with clients tells them what they are going to do first and how. It allows scheduling of the event. For example:

1) Get all bills together

2) Sort by type

3) Sort by date

4) Insert in file

5) File alphabetically

If the task is large you may have to break it down into smaller, more manageable steps over time.

Objective, Tools, and Steps (OTS) Form

Use this tool to help you move through the Objective, Tools and Steps (OTS) process.

OTS Form

Objective
What do you want to accomplish?

_____

_____

_____

_____

Tools
What things will you need to help you organize?

_____

_____

_____

_____

Steps
State the steps of the plan. What will you do? When will you do it? How long should it take?

1. _____

_____

2. _____

_____

3. _____

_____

4. _____

_____

5. _____

_____

3.2.5 The C.O.P.E. Strategy

As a professional organizer, you must help clients determine the placement of their things. You will help them to move, rearrange, and reorder what they have into systems that are both organized and workable.

Determining the placement of things is an active mental process. Without specific thought going into the placement of each item, the result is just rearranged disorder. This is one of the reasons that some clients you work with will tell you they hate to organize, or feel they can't do it — they feel overwhelmed with decisions. An easy way to help clients through this process is to teach them to "C.O.P.E.":

Category
Order
Proximity
Ease of Use

Using the principles in the C.O.P.E. method will help you to teach them easily and quickly how to move through a complicated process of decision making.

Category

Principle: Items that can be, should be sorted into groups.

The principle of categorization is a rather simple one — in fact, most people have been doing it since toddlerhood. So many toys are based on understanding how to classify objects — that is, how to place them into groups based on similarities. What they are doing is constructing categories of things.

Once a category is determined, subcategories can be determined, too. For example, the client's books can be categorized by genre – mystery novels, romance novels, etc. – but depending on the number of items in a category, individual items may be hard to find easily. As a subcategory, moving all the Rex Stout books into the same place might make sense for the mystery lover, or moving the Danielle Steel books into the same place might make sense for the romance enthusiast.

The ways to organize a category include creating subcategories based on a classification, and categorizing by type (color, shape, size, etc.). Remember, the categories must make sense to the client, not just to you.

Order

Principle: Groups of items that can be, should be placed in order within their group.

Moving forward with the same example, the romance enthusiast can further organize her books by putting them into alphabetical order by author, and then within categories of individual authors, she can alphabetize them again by title. The same holds true for spices, or files in an office, or an address book.

Some ways to order include:

- Ordering by size (ascending or descending order)

- Ordering from low to high (numerical order)

- Ordering by the alphabet (alphabetical order)

- Anything that works for the client

Proximity

Principle: Frequently used items should be placed the closest.

One of the most important principles of organization involves having what is needed (or liked, or used) the most the closest. How near something is depends on its value to the client to whom it belongs.

Take the book enthusiast's library, for example. The books she uses most frequently should be placed the closest to her. If she is a writer, she might have her reference books on a shelf closest to her desk. This principle is based on two things — personal value, and frequency of use.

Ease of Use

Principle: Items should be placed to be used easily.

The final concept in C.O.P.E. is ease of use. An electric appliance nowhere near an outlet isn't placed well. Similarly, a kitchen appliance used frequently but stored in the topmost cupboard in a kitchen is also in the wrong spot.

To determine ease of use placement, you must first help clients decide how often items are used. Frequently used items should be placed so they can be conveniently used. This principle increases in necessity based on how complex it is to prepare the item for use.

Consider a child's video game that must be hooked into a television each time it is used. If it is used every day, it should be placed where it can remain ready for use without setting it up each time. If it is a treat for once a week, it should be stored away out of sight. The principle of ease of use saves prep time and frustration because things are in place and ready to go.

3.3 Organizing the Individual

Organizing people is all about understanding the way people think. The mental processes that allow people to schedule and complete tasks, to track information, or to plan ahead — all of these are mental forms of organization.

An organized mind is the first step to achieving an organized environment. Author Wayne Dyer wrote a book called *You'll See it When You Believe It*. The premise of the book was that people must make a mental change before they see physical changes manifest in their lives. Dyer's theory also holds true for organization — before people can have organized surroundings and lives, there is some mental work to be done.

You may be called upon as a professional organizer to help people get organized on a personal level. In this section you will learn how to organize the individual's priorities, goals, and time.

3.3.1 Personal Organization Assessment

To truly be able to help a client learn to organize himself mentally, you need to get a sense of where your client is in the mental process of organization. With every client there is a different starting point. Some are beginners, some are good at some things and not at others, and some are advanced organizers looking for a way to fine-tune their systems.

Some clients are very mentally organized, but haven't gotten to the physical space part of it yet. Others are living in what appears to be organization and they still can't find anything. Still others have what looks like a mess, but in fact is their own individual system. For example:

- A client might have a very organized calendar and schedule, but feels she is in a rut. Maybe she needs to determine her long-term goals and go through the process of determining tasks to attain them.

- Another client might be a highly motivated and creative individual who has a hundred projects going and can't figure out how she will get them done. This client may have a problem with time management.

- Another client might be generally lost. He may not have a system that is working at home or at work. He might be chronically late, missing deadlines, and not even sure what time to pick up his children from school. This client might need some help managing his priorities.

Use the organizational assessment on the next few pages in two ways — first, to help you think about your own level of personal organization, and secondly as a tool for client assessment.

TIP: If you are using this as a handout at a seminar, or as a diagnostic tool, include a space at the bottom for the person's name, contact number, and ask them to indicate if they are interested in being contacted about their organizational needs based on your assessment of their results.

Personal Organizational Assessment

KEY: **A** = Always

U = Usually

S = Sometimes

R = Rarely

Attitudes and Actions

1. I feel more comfortable with a plan of some sort.   A   U   S   R

2. I make time to get organized.   A   U   S   R

3. I feel better about myself when I am organized.   A   U   S   R

4. I get annoyed when my house is a mess.   A   U   S   R

5. I am proud of my house.   A   U   S   R

6. People can be invited into my house with little or no stress or preparation.   A   U   S   R

7. Other people see me as organized.   A   U   S   R

8. I feel in control of my life.   A   U   S   R

9. I feel like I know what I'm doing.   A   U   S   R

10. I'm comfortable with my current level of organization.   A   U   S   R

11. I feel relaxed.   A   U   S   R

12. My family communicates and agrees about our level of organization.   A   U   S   R

13. My family goes to annually scheduled medical and dental check-ups.   A   U   S   R

14. I get an oil change for my vehicles regularly.   A   U   S   R

Goals

1. I know what I am doing in the next month.   A   U   S   R

2. I set short-term goals.   A   U   S   R

3. I set long-term goals.   A   U   S   R

4. I like to achieve results.   A U S R

5. I have something to show for my work in the last month.   A U S R

6. I complete projects I am proud of.   A U S R

7. I can measure my results.   A U S R

8. I do what I promise to do.   A U S R

9. I know what my priorities are.   A U S R

10. I don't waste time doing unimportant things.   A U S R

11. I know the priorities of my loved ones.   A U S R

12. I know how to break a large task into smaller parts.   A U S R

13. I use a to-do list.   A U S R

14. I am making progress.   A U S R

Time

1. I have a watch and I wear it.   A U S R

2. I know what I am doing this afternoon.   A U S R

3. I normally plan my weekends.   A U S R

4. I use a calendar for my work.   A U S R

5. I have a calendar with family events on it.   A U S R

6. I know my schedule and the schedule of my family members.   A U S R

7. I feel like I have enough time to do what I need to do every day.   A U S R

8. I don't feel rushed.   A U S R

9. I'm not overscheduled.   A U S R

10. My kids don't have too much to do.   A U S R

11. I spend time with my family.   A U S R

12. I'm usually on time to events.   A U S R

13. I remember my appointments.   A U S R

14. I get enough sleep.   A U S R

KEY: **A** = Always

U = Usually

S = Sometimes

R = Rarely

Information

1.	I can find my keys right now instantly.	A	U	S	R
2.	I know where my Social Security card is.	A	U	S	R
3.	I have the number to call my credit card companies in case my purse or wallet gets stolen.	A	U	S	R
4.	I can find my own and my spouse's and children's birth certificates.	A	U	S	R
5.	My checkbook is balanced.	A	U	S	R
6.	I pay my bills on time.	A	U	S	R
7.	I know where my important stuff is.	A	U	S	R
8.	I keep a personal phone book and I know where it is.	A	U	S	R
9.	I know where I keep my insurance policies and agent information.	A	U	S	R
10.	I know what homework my child has and if it's done.	A	U	S	R
11.	I have a place for my mail.	A	U	S	R
12.	I keep my tax records in order.	A	U	S	R
13.	I shred personal documents.	A	U	S	R
14.	I check my credit report annually.	A	U	S	R

Interpreting the Assessment

To determine your results, add up your score for each section individually using the following point key. Keep your results separate for each area of assessment.

Look at the chart on the facing page to quantify your scores for each section and identify the areas of organization you need to work on.

Answer	Points
Always	6
Usually	4
Sometimes	2
Rarely	0

If you mostly answered...	Then your score is...	And your level is...
Always	65-84 points	**Mastery**
Usually	45-64 points	**Acceptable**
Sometimes	23-44 points	**Developing**
Rarely	0-22 points	**Beginning**

Mastery

Mastery means that you have mastered the techniques of organizational skill and that you are currently putting them to use in your life with excellent results on a consistent basis. It is possible (and likely) that you may have achieved mastery in one area of the assessment and not another.

Acceptable

Acceptable means that you have mastered many of the techniques of organizational skill and that you are usually putting them to use in your life with good results on a fairly consistent basis. Is it possible for someone to achieve the level of "acceptable" and need to go no further? Yes, but it depends on their goals in this organizational area of their life.

Developing

Developing means that you have mastered some of the techniques of organizational skill, and that you are occasionally putting them to use in your life with fair results, on an irregular basis.

Beginning

Beginning means that you have mastered almost none of the techniques of organizational skill and that you are rarely putting them to use in your life with good results on a consistent basis — this level may identify new clients who have not worked with a professional organizer who consider themselves to have urgent organizational needs.

3.3.2 Determining Priorities

The first step in personal organization is to help clients clarify their priorities. So many books and so much media attention is paid to time management, that some people think the best way to start personal organization is to rush out and buy a day planner and some highlighters. Without first establishing priorities, goals have no context.

Think about this: If clients organize their time effectively to achieve goals that didn't really matter much in the first place, they might manage their time well, but they still don't end up achieving what they really want.

Priorities are simply those things in life that are valued the most. Clients might say their families are their number-one priorities. A new business owner may say her new business is her number-one priority. Realize that priorities change over time and need to be reviewed. For example, a college senior might say his studies are his number-one priority, but after graduation that will change.

Clients who want to set goals should make sure that they are in alignment with their life priorities. Consider the following common priorities your clients will state. What order would you put them in for yourself?

Think of a close friend, and imagine what her priorities might be:

- Career

- Family

- Home

- Health

- Money

- Relationships

- Leisure

- Religion

TIP: Some professional organizers use an "Epitaph Exercise" to help their clients zero in on the things they value the most. Clients are asked what values they would like to be known for "eternally" in the form of an epitaph on their tombstone.

Once your client has assessed his or her priorities, you can help them to set goals that balance their top priorities with the demands of everyday life. For example, if a client values spiritual life greatly, you would help him or her set a schedule that allowed time for religious reflection and spiritual growth.

3.3.3 Setting Goals

Personal organization requires clients to do a little soul searching and a little practical planning. To have a truly effective life you need to figure out where you want to go and how you plan to get there. A professional organizer may be required to help clients set clear, motivating, and do-able goals, and determine the tasks necessary to achieve them.

Goals are simple things, although they may not seem so at first. Goals are targets, the things clients want most to achieve. Once clients' goals are decided, plans to achieve them can be created. There are two basic types of goals:

- Short-term goals can be accomplished in a short time period and take relatively few tasks to complete.

- Long-term goals are the more complex goals that will take more time to accomplish.

In personal goal-setting, no matter what kinds of goals are being set, the order of steps to be followed is always the same.

1. Determine the Goal.

Ask clients about their ultimate achievable results, or best-possible scenarios. Have them carefully consider what their goals should be, and then write powerful goal statements, as explained below.

2. Consider the Tasks.

Clients' goals will have series of tasks required to achieve the end results. To determine tasks, have clients think about everything they will have to do, from the smallest to the most labor-intensive tasks, and plan them out.

3. Add the Time Component.

Goals must be managed over time. Help clients to schedule the projected completion dates for goals. This way they can allow for the necessary time to complete all the steps required to attain their goals.

Making a Goal Statement

Have clients begin by thinking about their ultimate goals. What do they want to accomplish? What are their best outcomes? Consider that goal statements should be:

Powerful

Goal statements should be high-energy, powerful statements that pull clients back on task every time they forget where they are and help them to remain focused.

Programmed

Good goal statements should be planned according to set schedules, and state projected achievement dates, whether that is in a week, a month, or five years.

Precise

Goal statements must be specific and contain precise information about what clients are doing, and when. Vague goal statements will not be motivating… or sometimes even understandable!

Practical

Finally, goals have to be practical. If clients aren't realistic they can set themselves up for failure. Good goal statements should be something that clients feel in their hearts are doable if they complete the necessary steps.

For example, we'll work with the following sample goal statement in Chapter 4 when you plan your business:

My goal is to…
"Open my own highly successful, lucrative professional organizing business called Serenity Solutions in which I specialize in serving residential clients with all aspects of their home organization needs, write articles and books, and become a locally known public speaker by eight months from today's date."

Goal Statement Form

Remember: A goal statement should be powerful, programmed, precise and practical.

To draft your goal statement, first start with the simple, fill-in sentence: My goal is to *[do what specific thing]*, by *[when]*.

My goal is to:

_____

_____

By:

_____

Now add words that will make your goal powerful and motivating. Consider words that add excitement and description to your goal. If your sentence makes you see it and feel it, you are on the right track.

My goal is to:

_____

_____

_____

_____

Now rewrite your goal on a small index card, and place it where you will see it every day.

Long-Term Goal Planner

What major goals would you like to accomplish...

...In One Year?

Career and Business Goals:

_____

_____

_____

_____

_____

Personal and Family Goals:

_____

_____

_____

_____

_____

...In Five Years?

Career and Business Goals:

_____

_____

_____

_____

_____

Personal and Family Goals:

_____

_____

_____

_____

_____

Planning to Achieve Goals

Unless clients plan the process step-by-step, they are leaving their goals to chance. Achieving a goal is simple, once the tasks necessary to get there are determined. To do this, clients need to set major tasks and smaller or mini-tasks that allow them to reach their major tasks.

Major tasks are big accomplishments — milestones along the way toward goals. For example, if a client is reorganizing his whole office, then a major task might be getting one of his filing cabinets completely organized. Once clients have determined all the major tasks that add up to their ultimate goals, they can move forward with determining the smaller or mini-tasks required to complete major tasks.

This is a straightforward process — just follow these steps:

- Set the goal as detailed above

- Write down the major tasks on the *Major Tasks Planner* (see the next page)

- Put the tasks in chronological order

- Fill out the *Task Breakdown Worksheet* (see the next page) to determine the minor tasks

- Estimate the time that each minor task will take to complete, and add the time for all the minor tasks to arrive at a tentative completion time for a major task

- Add the total times for the completion for each major task and you will have an estimated time for the ultimate goal

- Create a master schedule and calendar to determine what to do when

After determining the smaller tasks and their estimated times, have clients go back to the major task worksheets and fill in total estimated times for major tasks and milestones. Add these together to determine estimated times it will take for clients to complete their ultimate goals.

Major Tasks Planner

Ultimate Goal:

Major tasks needed to complete goal:

1. _____
2. _____
3. _____
4. _____
5. _____

Task Breakdown Worksheet

Major Task #1 Description:

Smaller Tasks:

Estimated Completion Time:

1. _____   _____
2. _____   _____
3. _____   _____
4. _____   _____
5. _____   _____

Total Estimated Time: _____

Total Estimated Cost: _____

Notes:

_____

_____

_____

You will want to repeat this format for every major task listed on the *Major Tasks Planner*.

3.3.4 Time Management

In the last 20 years, time management has been one of the most dominant self-help themes in books, articles, seminars, and websites. Even a new professional organizer may have a small library on the subject. This section is intended as an overview of the major elements of time management, with suggested ways to effectively help your clients.

Many clients are frustrated because they feel they don't have enough hours in the day to accomplish the things they really need to do. They know that less important stuff is chewing up their days. These clients may be falling behind in their work or putting in lots of late extra hours because they can't accomplish their goals during the standard work day. The phone rings too much; they are drowning in email; or they get too burned out to finish the job so they zone out in front of the television or their home computer.

There is a solution to all this frustration, and you can help your clients find it.

Find Out How Time Is Spent

The first step is to help your clients understand is how their time is currently being spent, so have clients log their daily routines for two weeks. Why two weeks? Because it takes a two-week period to view the variances in clients' current schedules. Have clients keep track of their major activities in hour, or even half-hour sized bites. You can use the *Time Activity Log* form provided on the next page.

> **TIP:** Don't let clients fill out their time logs at the end of the day or the end of the week.

Ask clients to commit to filling it in throughout the day, or they will have trouble remembering everything later on.

Notice that the Time Activity Log includes evenings and weekends. This is an intentional reminder that clients have all their waking hours to accomplish their goals. In addition to the daily work schedule, they need to plan for their family time, relaxation time, and exercise routines.

Time Activity Log

	SUN	MON	TUE	WED	THU	FRI	SAT
A.M.							
12:00							
1:00							
2:00							
3:00							
4:00							
5:00							
6:00							
7:00							
8:00							
9:00							
10:00							
11:00							
P.M.							
12:00							
1:00							
2:00							
3:00							
4:00							
5:00							
6:00							
7:00							
8:00							
9:00							
10:00							
11:00							

Using the results from your clients' log sheets, fill out the *Time Activity Summary* below to summarize each day's events. (Feel free to change the example categories on the left hand column on the form.)

What does the *Time Activity Summary* tell you? Perhaps it will tell you that nothing needs fixing. Look at your client's priorities and goals. Do they want to spend time with their families? How much time in a week is reasonable? Maybe they have the right amount of time allocated already and they just need advice to spend their time in more productive ways.

You can also ask your clients how typical those weeks were for them. If they have enough indicators to make you think that the information is skewed, ask your clients to fill in the forms for another week and try again.

On the other hand, changes might be needed in your clients' schedules to make room for their priorities. Discuss the amount of time that each category demands from your clients daily. Work with clients to select target times or percentages that make more sense for them and align with their goals.

Time Activity Summary

	SUN	MON	TUES	WED	THURS	FRI	SAT
Sleeping							
Commuting							
Productive Work							
Cooking/Cleaning							
Eating							
Studying/Homework							
Phone Calls							
Distractions							
Internet							
Video Games							
Television							
Email							
Grooming							
Family Time							
Exercise							
Social							

Time-Saving Tips

No one can make more than 24 hours happen in a day, but there are ways to help frustrated clients find more time in their day for the important things than they have now. In general, look for things to eliminate, ways to reschedule, and opportunities to combine activities. It is important that clients start to feel the power they have over their days. Consider these common time management problems and suggestions, and keep an expanded list of your own.

Too Much Time Commuting

Consider avoiding the worst part of rush hour or start the day by leaving for work 30 minutes earlier and going home 30 minutes earlier. A commute can be shortened dramatically by avoiding peak traffic times.

Too Much TV Time

A client might consider videotaping or using TiVo to control what day and time a favorite program is watched. He can also skip through the commercials!

Need More "Quiet Time" at Work

See if the client's employer allows for flex-scheduling. Many companies allow employees to work eight 9-hour days and one 8-hour day every two-week payroll period, with one additional day off. That gives the client an extra hour each day when the phones aren't ringing to concentrate on those pressing tasks that need to get done.

Need More Free Time

Many employers now offer a 4-by-10 plan, which could allow your client to put in a 40-hour week in 4 days. That gives a client a 3-day weekend every week to get those big chores done.

Too Much Time on the Phone

Does a client need to call someone who loves to talk? Suggest he have a piece of paper handy with conversation cues to keep them on track. By staying on track a gabby caller won't ruin your client's time management plan.

Too Much Time Doing Chores

What is your client's time really worth? Is it well spent on hours of lawn care, laundry, housecleaning, or car maintenance? Evaluate what chores around the house can be done as well or better by professionals and whether or not it is worth the price to hire someone else to do the work and free the client to do those things that are more important.

'ABC' To-Do Lists

In a previous section, you saw how to teach your clients to turn their goals into doable tasks. Those smaller tasks listed on the *Task Breakdown Worksheet* can be used to make up your clients' to-do lists.

But what if you have a client who has 45 items on their to-do list? The answer is simply to put first things first. Prioritize. Have the client go through the to-do list and mark each item with an A, B, or C:

- "A" things must be done first in chronological order, or are those items that potentially will deliver the greatest benefit to the clients' lives.

- "B" things are important to do, but in the larger picture, they are not urgent.

- "C" things can logically happen later or are merely "nice-to-have" instead of "must-have now."

    TIP: Remember that priorities change over time. The A-B-C markings should be reviewed monthly to see if they still reflect the clients' goals.

Now clients actually start to control what happens in their day. Have clients use the *Time Activity Log* sheet provided, and use it as a weekly planner. Start by filling in the parts of their daily routine that are unavoidable, such as grooming, commuting, standing meetings, and scheduled classes. Everywhere else, clients can work on their to-do lists. Have them start filling in the blank time on a calendar with A-list to-do items. When the A-list items are complete, move on to the B-list items, and then eventually take on the C-list tasks.

> **TIP:** Far too often, clients remember to schedule deadlines when things are due — but not the work itself needed to complete the tasks. Remind them that it is more valuable to schedule work than reminders for when goals should be met.

Tell your clients that if they don't complete tasks as scheduled, then they must change tomorrow's schedule and put it back to deal with until completed. Keep the highest priority items on the top of the list at all times.

Personal Organizing Products

Coach your clients that the routine of prioritizing, planning, and performing the work is the most important element of time management. When it comes to managing time, PDAs don't have much on the old paper-based personal calendar. The important thing is that they start using some kind of organizer, and stay with it.

It is very important to maintain only one calendar. If a client uses a digital handheld organizer and desktop computer software calendar, be sure that they are synchronized daily. If the family maintains another calendar at home, keep it synchronized with the personal calendar. Too many calendars with different information cause miscommunication and disorganization.

The Day Planner

There is no shortage of personal day organizer products on the market, which are all quite similar. Have your clients flip through several brands and decide what feels right for them and reflects personal taste.

Computer Calendars

Today, all the major business-oriented email software packages contain a calendar utility for scheduling appointments and reminders. If your clients have access to this software, be sure to suggest they use the application to schedule appointments with themselves to work on their to-do lists.

PDAs

A large assortment of affordable Personal Digital Assistants (PDAs) are on the market and your clients may choose to manage their calendars using that technology. They should allow clients to synchronize their calendars with the calendar maintained on their desktop computers, as well as Internet access and email utilities. Note that clients should spend their money only on features they will really use. Gadgets and features eventually provide more distractions and challenges than benefits in time management.

Celebrating Success

Just like quitting smoking, getting out of debt, or losing weight, when clients take control of the way they use their time, it is cause for celebration. Old habits, even bad ones, are hard to break. One well-known and successful behavior modification technique is to reinforce good behavior with a reward system. Especially in the fragile, early days of learning a new routine, convince clients to commit to rewarding themselves for staying on track.

Perhaps a client should buy that new CD they have been thinking about as a reward for filling out the weekly planner for a whole month. Encourage a client to take their spouse out to a concert, a picnic, or a special dinner to reward both of them for their efforts and mutual support of each other. Advise the parents of a child who stayed with a new homework schedule for a month to find a suitable pleasing reward.

3.4 Organizing the Home

"Clutter is anything that isn't supportive to your environment. If it isn't supportive to your environment, then why are you holding on to it? On the other hand, you don't have to throw everything out to be organized. You can have collections, but they need to have a spot."

— Brenda Clements, Professional Organizer

Professional organizers who help clients organize their homes call themselves "residential specialists." They help clients with every aspect of home organization in each room in the house, and determine systems and procedures — even helping clients get their families organized as well.

Every home is different, and the inhabitants in homes differ, too. There are people who live alone, those who are married or sharing their lives with partners, some who are married with children, and "empty nesters" who are learning to live in two-person households again. How people live and who they live with often determines how they organize their space.

Use the information provided here as a guide for helping clients organize their homes. But remember, this information is only a basic discussion — you will have to use your own creativity and organizational skills in each client situation to respond to their specific needs.

3.4.1 Defining Home Organization

How things get out of hand, and how living spaces get cluttered and disorganized, is a mystery to many people. Things might start out orderly and disintegrate over time, or perhaps from the first day a family moves into a new space it doesn't seem to work well.

People living in a disorganized space might define it as any (or all) of the following:

- Too small

- Crowded

- A mess

- Disorderly

- Ugly

- Cluttered

- Hard to clean

- Annoying

- Hard work

- Stressful

- Impossible

A home should be a place of rest and rejuvenation and beauty. It should be a place for love and happiness and celebration. It should be a place they can't wait to get back to every day. It should be a haven.

People living in disorganized, cluttered spaces just don't get the same benefit of renewal that those who live in beautiful, well-ordered places do. This is why clients use professional organizers to help them with their living spaces. They don't have the haven they want — and they want to change it.

So what is the perfect home? What will best suit the personal tastes, daily activities and responsibilities, and personality and family's needs? For most people, it is defined as a mix of the following four traits, in a balance that is individual to them:

- Functional

- Beautiful

- Detailed

- Uncomplicated

Try the *Home Attitudes Quiz* on the next few pages for fun, and then use it as a tool with your clients to find out their personal preferences for a perfect home.

The Home Attitudes Quiz

Answer the questions below with A, B, C, or D (choose the one that is MOST like you); then use the answer key at the end of the quiz to help you determine your personal home attitude.

1. **When you visit Disneyland with your family for the first time, the thing you find most amazing is:**

   A) The comfortable California weather

   B) The minute elements and workmanship in the Pinocchio ride

   C) How they efficiently handle such a big crowd on a daily basis

   D) The gorgeous scenery in the "Soaring Over California" attraction

2. **The thing you admire the most about your best friend's car is:**

   A) The amazing electronics and global positioning feature

   B) The racy red color and convertible top

   C) All the little extras that make it convenient and useful

   D) The smooth ride

3. **On a "museum vacation" with your family, you gravitate toward:**

   A) The art museum

   B) The miniature museum

   C) The aerospace museum

   D) The Zen gardens

4. **You go back to school to take some classes that interest you. You sign up for:**

   A) Accounting for Business

   B) The Ins and Outs of Home Repair

   C) Watercolor Painting of Outdoor Landscapes

   D) Simplifying Your Life

5. **When you choose a place to eat, you look for:**

   A) A lovely French restaurant

   B) A lakeside restaurant

   C) The local "home-cooking" restaurant

   D) A cafeteria or buffet-style eatery

6. **Your morning skin cleansing routine consists of:**

   A) Soap and water

   B) An all-in-one skin cleansing system, conveniently placed in your shower

   C) A product derived from rose extract, packaged in an attractive set of bottles

   D) A five-part special cleansing program, applied morning and night

7. **Your bedroom wallpaper choice would be:**

   A) One color, slightly textured, in a neutral shade

   B) Landscape paper with a garden motif

   C) Washable, stain-resistant floral pattern

   D) One that features reproductions of famous paintings

8. **Your idea of a peaceful Saturday afternoon alone at home is:**

   A) Taking a well-deserved nap

   B) Putting together a jigsaw puzzle

   C) Arranging a display of flowers for your table

   D) Fixing the screen door

9. **People comment on your Christmas tree every year. This is because it:**

   A) Is natural and tasteful, with no garish lights or tinsel

   B) Is a technological marvel, complete with a handy light timer

   C) Has four generations' worth of ornaments, gathered from all over the world

   D) Perfectly complements the room and fits perfectly in front of the window

10. You won $1,000! You buy:

A) A tune-up and detail for your car

B) An upgrade for your computer

C) A sculpture from a new local artist you admire

D) Nothing — it's going right into the bank

Answer Key

Using the key on the next page, see how many answers you have in each category. After you have determined this read the explanation for each of the categories below. If you score highly in two categories, take into account how both of these home attitude areas will enter into your home organizational style.

1. A – Uncomplicated
   B – Detailed
   C – Functional
   D – Beautiful

2. A – Functional
   B – Beautiful
   C – Detailed
   D – Uncomplicated

3. A – Beautiful
   B – Detailed
   C – Functional
   D – Uncomplicated

4. A – Detailed
   B – Functional
   C – Beautiful
   D – Uncomplicated

5. A – Detailed
   B – Beautiful
   C – Uncomplicated
   D – Functional

6. A – Uncomplicated
   B – Functional
   C – Beautiful
   D – Detailed

7. A – Uncomplicated
   B – Beautiful
   C – Functional
   D – Detailed

8. A – Uncomplicated
   B – Detailed
   C – Beautiful
   D – Functional

9. A – Uncomplicated
   B – Functional
   C – Detailed
   D – Beautiful

10. A – Detailed
    B – Functional
    C – Beautiful
    D – Uncomplicated

Functional Living

You like the objects around your home to serve a purpose. If something is out, there is a reason for it — you use it. You like clever organizing solutions and making good use of space. You also like gadgets, technology, and machines. Your home should have everything set up so it's ready to go — your electronics, your home entertainment center, your tool shed. It all has to be ready to plug in and turn on.

Detailed Living

You are a collector. Maybe you have memorabilia, or family heirlooms, or Mickey Mouse watches — whatever it is, you need a nice way to display it that keeps it safe, looking good, and organized. You appreciate intricate workmanship and you like things that have a lot of pieces or parts, which you organize in your own way. You can be meticulous.

Uncomplicated Living

No muss, no fuss is your motto. You like to keep things simple. You appreciate comfort and ease, and you don't like a lot of fussy details. You enjoy space, you like to be surrounded in comfort, and you like to feel like you can kick back and enjoy yourself in your home. You may be social and enjoy entertaining, or spend a lot of quality time with family — but whatever you do, you want to have a relaxed atmosphere while you do it.

Beautiful Living

You love to have people see your home, and you spend a lot of time on it. You have fresh flowers, you enjoy art, you may invite others over for dinner or cocktail parties, and you love to entertain. You may have had an interior designer work with you in your home, or you would like to if you could. You may have antiques or other expensive things in your home.

Simple quizzes like this one will help you establish information about a trend in your living and taste, but shouldn't be considered a complete diagnostic tool. However, by using this quiz you may be able to tune into what is important to you, and how it will affect your organizational plans.

3.4.2 Home Organizing Products

There are hundreds of thousands of organizing products on the market, which you will choose from and recommend to clients. Most of these will be space-saving devices, storage units, ease-of-access devices, or computer software. Over time you will start to develop favorite product lines or manufacturers, which will be the "product toolbox" you go to when you are problem-solving.

You can begin to develop your product toolbox as you read this chapter. There are product links listed for every room in the house. Where links are provided, click on them to explore what is offered. You will also find more resources at the end of this guide.

If it looks like a product or line of products you would choose or recommend, add it to your "favorites" website list as a bookmark. Just open the "bookmarks" or "favorites" function on your browser, and make a folder in your favorites list called Product Toolbox.

You can also put yourself on store or manufacturer mailing lists and request copies of recent catalogs and brochures that you can keep in your reference library or share with clients. Often you can sign up to be added to their mailing lists and new product announcements right on their websites.

Using a Bot to Keep Up

No mere mortal can keep up with the Internet, so why not use an Internet organizing application called a bot? At **www.BotSpot.com** you can find an assortment of applications that will search the Internet for any changes to a list of websites you choose. There are also bots that will search news reports and press releases for information on keywords that you select, such as "organize" and "organizing."

3.4.3 Planning, Purging and Storing

In each room or area of a client's life you organize, you will need to take three steps: planning, purging and storing. Let's revisit your techniques explained at the beginning of this chapter, and think about how you can use them to plan, purge, and store.

Planning

Use the Condition and Calamity concept to help clients with more than one area that needs organizing through a prioritizing exercise. This tool will help them to figure out what space (or area within a space) is the most pressing project. Once you have this information you will know how to prioritize their jobs.

Use the Objectives, Tools, and Steps concept as another planning tool. Clients can give you their objectives, but it is up to you to develop the steps that you will help them take, and the tools that they will need to achieve their organizational objectives. It will help you get a grip on the scope of the project, the client's true goals, and any products you'll need to purchase before you start to purge and store.

Purging

You can use the Minimize, Maximize and Maintain concept to help clients plan their home organization. What do they need less or fewer of? How can they maximize their space? You will need their input about how they want the space to serve them. Finally, you will leave them with a plan about how to maintain their organization when you leave.

Use the Treasure, Trash, Tools and Toys concept to help clients with piles of clutter to figure out what stays and what goes. This is where rolling up the sleeves and getting down to it is necessary.

Storing

The C.O.P.E. (Category, Order, Proximity, and Ease of Use) tool will help clients make sound decisions about how their "stuff" should be stored to give them the most benefit from their systems. The C.O.P.E. tool allows you to create useable systems in clients' spaces that will make it possible for them to use their belongings and their spaces to best advantage. Explain C.O.P.E. to your clients if they are having trouble wrapping their head around a system you are creating for them.

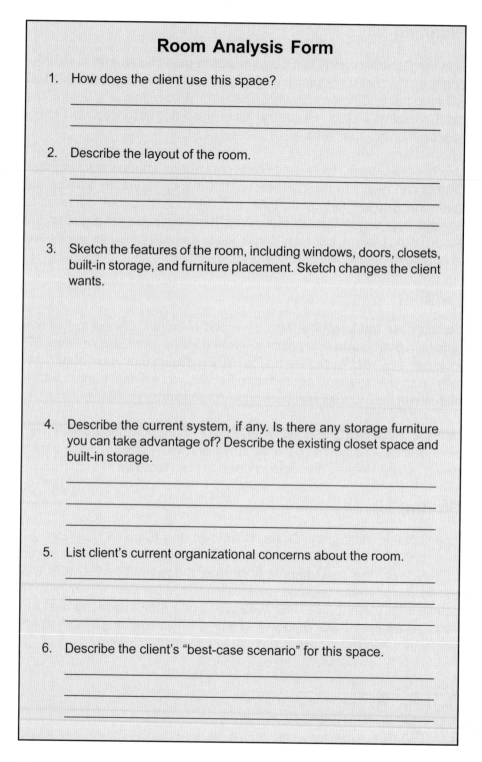

Room Analysis Form

1. How does the client use this space?

    _____

    _____

2. Describe the layout of the room.

    _____

    _____

    _____

3. Sketch the features of the room, including windows, doors, closets, built-in storage, and furniture placement. Sketch changes the client wants.

4. Describe the current system, if any. Is there any storage furniture you can take advantage of? Describe the existing closet space and built-in storage.

    _____

    _____

    _____

5. List client's current organizational concerns about the room.

    _____

    _____

    _____

6. Describe the client's "best-case scenario" for this space.

    _____

    _____

    _____

3.4.4 Documenting the Space

With a busy schedule and clients with big homes, you will need to take notes during consultations to record the details of the layouts, and the clients' comments and primary concerns about each space. When you are back at your office thinking through the planning stage before work appointments, you'll need to jog your memory with these notes.

Unless you are a skilled draftsperson, bring a camera with you as well to take a few pictures of each room. You'll be able to check on any details you may have missed in your notes.

> **TIP:** Ask clients for permission to take "before-and-after" pictures, which you can later use to demonstrate your excellent work — both in your portfolio of past projects, and on your website. Make this whole process infinitely easier by using a digital camera for easy uploading to your website.

Also, use a *Room Analysis Form* like the one on the facing page to help you take notes.

3.5 Organizing Each Room

Clients may be looking for help tackling their whole home, or one or two key areas of disorganization. Here is a room-by-room breakdown of organization ideas and concepts for you to study.

You can refer back to this guide when working with clients. Print this section of the ebook out (you can find a copy of the ebook on the CD-ROM), punch holes in it, and add it to a binder. In the binder, include blank sheets in each section so that you can add notes, magazine clippings and sketches of ideas to use as you grow your business and your talent.

3.5.1 Bedrooms

Bedrooms are probably the most personal space you will enter in clients' homes. Bedrooms are where people relax, let their hair down, and rejuvenate for the next day. And when you think about it, a bedroom is often where the majority of time at home is actually spent.

Bedroom Activities

Bedrooms may also be used to read, do needlepoint, talk on the phone, watch television, use laptops, read the Sunday paper, and sometimes even work. When this is the case, find out if this is a matter of choice or necessity for the client, and if they would like to move any of these activities into another space.

Many organizational experts believe that bedroom activities should be connected to relaxing and unwinding. They caution against bedroom offices, or televisions in bedrooms. While ultimately clients have to decide what works best for them, if they don't find their bedrooms relaxing, it will be your job to help them discover why and help them fix these problems.

Review these ideas for bedroom organization, and think about your own ideas to make clients' bedrooms relaxing and orderly living spaces.

Beds

Besides being the ultimate necessity in a bedroom, beds can provide extra storage space, too. Many beds are made with built-in storage features, but even if that isn't the case, most beds can accommodate under-the-bed storage.

Storage units made of plastic can be easily rolled under the bed and removed when needed. Flat plastic storage boxes with lids simply slide underneath the bed. Bed elevators – cone-shaped plastic, wood, or metal blocks – can elevate the bed and provide even more space for storage underneath.

Shelving units can be used behind a bed as an interesting headboard that doubles as more space for books and bedside or decorative items. Make sure to carefully secure any shelving unit used as a headboard to the wall before clients use them.

Bedroom Furniture

A handy way to get extra storage in the bedroom is to make sure that pieces of furniture in the bedroom have a double use. For example, bedside tables that are also chests of drawers instantly double their usefulness.

For bureaus and chests of drawers, there are inexpensive drawer inserts or dividers, which allow you to separate small items of clothing for easy viewing and instant access.

Remember that one of the most frustrating things about drawer storage is overcrowding. Remind clients to make sure that there aren't too many clothing items for each drawer. Clothing should be stacked loosely enough so that it doesn't wrinkle.

Armoires are excellent storage solutions because they close away items out of sight that detract from the overall feel of the bedroom, such as TVs or music systems not in use. Even an unused closet can double as an "armoire."

Closets

The primary source of storage in a bedroom – a well-organized closet – can make all the difference. The first and most important thing to do with a closet is minimize. Tell your clients about the One-Year Rule:

If you haven't worn it in one year, get rid of it.

Also, if you live in a climate that is either very cold or very hot for part of the year, you will have a variety of clothes that you will not use for a whole season. Consider storing these clothes out of the main closet area.

Help clients organize clothing by size (long and short items) and by color, or color range, for easy access. Make sure that all the pieces of one outfit are hung together.

When you are ready to organize the remaining items, get the right hardware. Sometimes the best solution for organizing a closet is a modular closet unit, which is a unit with various drawers and shelves that you place inside your closet to alter the storage options. At the very least, wire shelving units or additional rods can be added — an additional rod often allows double the number of clothes you can store in one space.

Make sure when you install rods or shelves that they are high enough off the ground. In general, clothing rods for dresses or coats should be at least 76 inches (192 cm) above the floor; a lower rod used for shirts and sport coats needs to be at least 36 inches (91.5 cm) from the floor. If you have a particularly tall client, you may want to measure some clothing to be sure.

The number of tools available to help you organize clients' closets today is astounding. You can get everything from hanger holders – which allow you to hang up to five hangers in the amount of space you would usually be able to hang only one – to hooks, over-the-door hanging storage systems, hanging shoe racks, and plastic, stackable containers for closet shelves. You can visit the websites below to see some samples of products and closet units.

- *California Closets*
  Call 1-800-274-6754
  www.calclosets.com

- *Closetmaid.com*
  www.closetmaid.com

- *Easy Closets.com*
  www.easyclosets.com

- *Easy Track — Do-it-Yourself Custom Storage*
  www.easytrack.com

- *Mills Pride*
  www.millspride.com

- *Rubbermaid, Inc.*
  Home Organization — Closets and Organizers
  www.rubbermaid.com

Children's Bedrooms

What if the bedroom you are helping a client organize is for a child? Then there are additional considerations to take into account. Making a child's bedroom something he or she can handle alone will save clients a world of time, and help children develop their own organizational skills.

Let your clients know that one of the best things they can do for their child is to make his or her living space something manageable. Of course, very small children will always need some help organizing and maintaining their bedrooms, but even a four-year-old can pick up and put away toys and games if they are stored in easy-to-reach locations.

Baby's Room

The rule of thumb for a baby's room is that everything should be easy to reach and accessible to exhausted new parents, but adequately protected from curious baby hands. Change tables often have storage space under them. Wicker baskets can be used to store quick-change items like diapers and undershirts that parents may need to grab with one hand. If there is room, many parents like to have a rocking chair in the corner for late-night feedings (put a table next to it for burp cloths, etc.).

You might also include a curio shelf up high to display mementos and figurines that are breakable. Most importantly, a baby's room must be safe — cover outlets, and ensure that blind strings are strangle-proof and that all windows are secured.

Child's Room

Frustrated parents can get to the point where they feel like they can't see their child through all the clutter in his or her room. Toys, games, puzzles, stuffed animals, school projects, craft materials, homework, musical instruments, collections, and just plain stuff can multiply rapidly. Your job as an organizer is to help clients make a space for their child that the child can maintain and at the same time is still cool and kid-friendly!

Consider toy boxes that sort multi-piece toys into colorful baskets, bulletin boards to display art work and certificates, and a dry-erase board on the door for communicating messages between parent and child. Make sure the child has a clutter-free and non-distracting place to do homework. Your clients can teach children to part with items they no longer use by donating them to the less fortunate, or simply store unused items in another space such as a basement or attic, out of the main living space.

Teen's Room

Warning — private space ahead! Teenagers are notorious for needing private space to chat on the phone, send online messages to friends, or just to be alone. With this highly independent age group, it takes tact to be able to help them organize. The best way to do this is to involve them in the process. Interact with them like you would an adult, and get their input on how they want to use their space. Teens (and older children) need to have some creative control if they are going to have responsibility for maintaining the system you create.

Guest Rooms

A guest room should be comfortable and easy to maintain. A guest room may not have to be a dedicated space — it can also make an excellent storage space, too. The trick is to manage the space so that it can be quickly transformed as needed to accommodate guests, and used effectively when guests aren't present.

Talk with clients about their expectations for their guest rooms. How often is it used for guests, what else is it used for, and so on? Items stored in guest rooms should not be things that are used frequently, and should still allow enough space to accommodate guests' luggage and belongings so those items don't spill out into the rest of clients' homes.

3.5.2 Bathrooms

Bathrooms are one of the most vital intersections in a home — one that contains all of clients' personal effects for bathing, grooming, and getting ready each day. Although bathrooms are usually created to be functional, there is no reason why a bathroom cannot be an extension of clients' personal spaces — and beautiful, too.

Bathrooms that are both organized and attractive spaces will help clients transition from wake-up to more positive workdays, as well as make wind-down times at the end of the day calmer. Tell clients to purge bathrooms weekly. This can be done while they empty the wastebaskets, or while supervising young kids in the bath (you're in there anyway). Toss the empty or almost-empty containers of shampoo, soap almost down to slivers, and do a quick once-over for medicine cabinets and makeup.

Counter Space

What you see in a bathroom when you walk inside should be attractive, functional, and uncluttered. Bathroom counters can be used for storage, but only for those items that can be attractively displayed.

Consider glass containers or other small, attractive storage containers for toiletry items and small soaps, small baskets for guest towels, attractive perfume bottles on a decorative tray, or scented candles (use small coasters or other protective mountings so that they don't destroy clients' counters when they burn).

Sink Area Drawers

Besides being a necessity in a bathroom, bathroom drawers are a place where clutter seems to multiply. But makeup, soaps, toiletries, lotions, and other items can all be stored effectively in bathroom drawers.

First, remember to help clients purge. Liquid makeup items should not be kept longer than six months; other makeup, a year. The same is true for lotions and face creams and other topical skin medicines and preparations. Make sure to remind clients to check the dates on these items before determining whether or not these stay or get thrown away.

Use small plastic organizing containers like trays inside drawers to organize contents. Even small Tupperware bowls (**www.tupperware.com**) or other flat plastic containers can be used to organize small items. Suggest to clients that extra storage containers no longer in use in the kitchen can move permanently into bathroom drawers as an inexpensive alternative to purchasing new bathroom organizing equipment!

You can also suggest divided plastic storage trays or even interlocking drawer organizers like those featured at The Container Store (**www. containerstore.com**).

Sink Area Cupboards

This is where you put the things guests aren't supposed to see. When organizing under-the-sink bathroom cupboards, remember to consider their depth. Using the proximity rule – that is, the most frequently used things are placed the closest – remember to place infrequently used items at the back of cupboards. Consider stackable clear plastic storage units for this space.

When clients' bathrooms don't have enough out-of-sight storage, a simple fabric skirt can be put up using Velcro on an unenclosed sink to instantly provide another out-of-sight storage space. Fabric can be chosen to match the décor of the bathroom for an attractive look.

Medicine Cabinet

Medicine cabinet organization is crucial to ensure medicines are easy to find when needed. Ask clients to consider designating one shelf for each bathroom user, and then organize medications on the shelf in the way that makes the most sense.

Some people with a variety of medications might choose to order these by category; others might alphabetize their medicines. There are a variety of medicine storage options, including daily pill box organizers.

Remember to remind clients to make sure to dispose of old medicines, which can be both ineffective and unsafe. People have a funny habit of hanging onto prescription medicine "just in case."

Bathtub or Shower Area

Remind clients that keeping things organized in the bathtub or shower area not only makes the area look far more attractive but also can prevent injury. Shower caddies can be a functional way to house all of the bottles of shampoo, conditioner, shaving preparations, and soap that find their way into showers and tubs. Some of these fit directly over the shower or tub faucet, others are mounted to the walls of the shower or bathtub by suction or adhesive.

You can keep kids' bath toys all in one space and let them dry properly with an inexpensive net that attaches to the wall with suction cups (these are sold at kids' specialty stores).

Freestanding or Portable Storage

In small or older homes, clients may still find themselves short on storage. What are some solutions you can offer?

Extra storage space can be added using an inexpensive shelving unit that fits above the back of the toilet, which can be purchased at any hardware store. Some units are suspended using metal poles that fit around the sides of the toilet, others are placed directly on the back of the toilet, and still others attach to the wall.

Talk with clients about using an extra bookcase or other shelving unit from another part of the house if they have one that will fit. Bracket any large freestanding unit to the wall if there is any chance it might tip over.

Portable cabinets and rolling drawer units can be an excellent resource in a bathroom area. One professional organizer interviewed for this guide helped a client pick out an attractive plastic storage cabinet for her bathroom. The client, who was artistic, used stencils and paint to decorate the unit and coordinate it with her bathroom. Total cost: about $25. You can find suitable units at online stores like Lillian Vernon (**www.lillian vernon.com**), or in your local home or hardware store.

3.5.3 Kitchens

You've probably noticed that people naturally gravitate towards a kitchen. Feeding ourselves is an elemental need, but keep in mind that there is so much more involved in a wonderful kitchen than sustenance. Kitchens should be places where people feel nurtured and welcomed. They should provide the workstation for cozy dinners, family get-togethers and glorious holidays.

The key to helping clients with kitchens is to help them find their own workable systems that are unique to their patterns of living and kitchen function. A kitchen should be organized in a way that makes the cook in the family happy – or at least keep them sane – with a functional space that offers everything within reach. There is nothing more frustrating than needing a specific tool for a well-timed recipe and not being able to find it. Here are some tips for making the kitchen work well for your client.

Counter Space

Kitchen counter space must do two things. First, it must be functional, as in enough clear counter space to make meal preparation easy. Breadboxes and canisters can make attractive counter space storage, but they should leave enough room to use.

> **TIP:** Some decorative containers are not meant to house food-stuffs and contain lead in their painted surfaces. Make sure that the storage canisters are food-appropriate.

Secondly, counters should provide storage space for appliances used daily. If there is little space or a number of appliances, some may be mounted underneath cabinets. Other appliances that are used weekly or less frequently can be housed in kitchen cupboards.

Cupboards and Pantries

Kitchen cupboards can be used for anything from plates, cups, and glasses to canned and boxed foods and spices. You can help clients arrange their cupboards using the two-step rule: you should never have to move more than two steps to get what you need. To make this possible, organize the kitchen cupboards by category, and make sure that everything needed for specific and frequent tasks is housed in the same area.

Kitchen pantries are often just like large closet spaces – and they can be just as unorganized. But unlike clothes closets, the contents of a pantry can expire. It's important for clients to be able to see what they have and have easy access to pantry contents.

Clients will feel more organized and ahead of the game if they can learn to shop one step ahead, by always having extra of frequently used items on hand. For example, when the catsup runs out they take the "backup bottle" out of the pantry, and add it to the shopping list. This way you are seldom truly "out" of an item.

For deep or inaccessible pantries or cupboards, consider some pantry hardware. Multi-shelf lazy susans can be installed to provide a turntable device on each shelf that rotates to see pantry items easily, and pantry slides are pull-out shelving units that move in and out to allow pantry contents to be viewed. You can review some of the options you'll have to offer your clients at **www.rockler.com** (do a search for "pantries").

Stackable plastic storage boxes can protect dry foods and maximize the use of space, and wire baskets, bins, and shelving racks also help keep things organized and accessible.

> **TIP:** You should set up a reminder system for clients to rotate their canned goods. That is, they should use up the oldest food first, especially if they keep an emergency stockpile of cans.

The Refrigerator

There are many space-saving and organizational gadgets that you can suggest to clients that fit right in the fridge to maximize space and create instant order, such as:

- Plastic soft drink can holders

- Refrigerator turntables or lazy Susans

- Stackable plastic containers for leftovers and other foods

- Space-saving plastic pitchers and water holders to maximize space

Teach your clients the best way to stock the fridge: items with the earliest expiration dates should be placed in front of those with later expiration dates, just like they do at a grocery store.

Also, remind clients to purge their refrigerators of old or expired food every week before they do their grocery shopping. This will also help clients plan for their shopping list as they review the contents of their refrigerator. You can also teach clients and their families to keep a running list right on the fridge of items they use the last of, so they can be repurchased at the next shop.

More Kitchen Storage

There are a wide variety of available products to organize and maximize kitchen space.

- Freestanding kitchen islands dramatically increase both storage and counter space. Many professional organizers swear by kitchen islands, and a free-standing one can be brought into a spacious kitchen instantly.

- Metal or wooden wall racks can be used to house spices, or with hooks to display potholders, aprons or even cutlery and kitchen tools.

- Ceiling-mounted racks can be an excellent way to organize pots and pans, out of the way but close enough in proximity for ease of use. Some racks have wire shelves attached to increase storage space.

- StemTrack is an under-the-cabinet track system that allows you to safely mount clients' glasses by the base the same way that some bars do. It adds to the overall look of the kitchen, maximizes unused space—and keeps the inside of glasses from getting dusty.

You can browse some of these items at Wal-Mart's web site at **www.wal-mart.com** (click on "For the Home," then "Storage & Organization," then "Kitchen").

3.5.4 Family/Living Rooms

Called the family or living room for obvious reasons, this room is the place where clients can put their feet up and enjoy some downtime with their families. Whether clients are watching DVDs with their kids, listening to music with friends, or even playing video games, the family room is probably the place they will do it.

Family room equipment should be easy to use, functional, and easily accessible. You will want to combine convenience with comfort for a healthy mix in this room. Having a way to organize the DVDs, the video games, and the CDs is of the utmost importance to clients. Having technological gadgets set up so they are efficient will help them enjoy the space to its potential.

Note that in some clients' homes, there will be a family room and a separate living room. In this case, the family room will be the one with the most traffic, while the living room will usually be reserved for special occasions. Living room space that is not used as often as family room space is a good place for display of breakable art, and collectables. Living rooms may also have additional space to house clients' libraries. The fact that the room has less traffic usually means that the organizing problems and clutter are reduced.

Furniture Placement and Function

To determine if the furniture placement is appropriate, talk with clients about their current setup. Can they get to everything they want to use? What are their biggest frustrations with their family rooms today? Is the furniture comfortable, or is there one chair everyone avoids? If so, it should be replaced.

Consider ways to add storage and definition to a room using better furniture placement. For example, a couch that is not placed against a wall can be used to back a small freestanding shelf unit. Make sure that the unit is level to the top of the couch and won't fall or tip over. This can be a good place to store books, videos, or other family room equipment. When the shelf is topped with several plants, it will help you to give a room a real sense of definition.

Coffee tables can double their usefulness if they have built-in storage drawers, or a hope chest or another chest with a lid can be used as an attractive coffee table. A large chest can be organized by inserting wooden drawer dividers or using plastic boxes that can be placed inside and lifted out. These can be used to store video games, board games, CDs and DVDs. Good choices for side tables are those that have extra shelves or better yet, drawers to store additional family room equipment.

Be careful about the placement of heavy entertainment centers and freestanding shelving. These should be secured to the wall to prevent tipping or falling. This is especially true in the case of clients with small children. If shelving units placed against walls are not sufficiently secure, the placement of shims under the corners of the bottom shelves can help.

Adequate Seating

One idea to help clients save space and still offer additional seating are stackable chairs. They can be stacked and stored, or used in the room and only stacked when needed to create extra room.

If clients need additional seating and have limited budgets, suggest that they add some decorative pillows that can be pulled up on the floor for kids and able-bodied adults to sit on and lean against. Pillows are also an effective way to brighten a room and add a little freshness without a gigantic investment. When not in use, pillows can be placed on a couch or in a decorative pile in a corner space.

Lighting

Unlike most other rooms in the house, the family room is usually designed without overhead lighting, so designing a lighting concept offers more creative freedom in this space. Lighting should be pleasant and bright, but also changeable for watching a movie or playing a board game. Place lighting so that outlets are in easy reach and so cords don't dangle or stretch across areas. You can browse lighting options at the client's favorite home decor outlet, or online at sites such as Lamps Plus (**www. lampsplus.com**).

Entertainment and Media Storage

Entertainment centers are the hub of a family room. They may simply house the television, or they may be multileveled shelving systems that also store CD and DVD players, speakers, video game consoles, and more.

There are many types of shelving units available for family rooms, from built-in wooden units, to those made with metal and glass. Shelving ranges in price and many shelving kits can be assembled after purchase. If clients have unused linen closets or hall closets adjacent to their family rooms this might be the perfect destination for video, DVD and CD storage.

- *Racks and Stands.com — Entertainment Centers*
  www.racksandstands.com

- *Organize.com — CD Storage*
  www.organize.com/cdstorage.html

Alphabetize music by artist, and movies by title. Some clients who are fans of certain actors may prefer to designate all their Tom Hanks or Julia Roberts movies as their own classifications.

Make sure couches are placed close enough to entertainment systems to see the TV and for video game cords to reach. You might suggest an audio/visual switcher to clients, which allows all the equipment to remain hooked up to the TV while clients switch back and forth between equipment at the turn of a dial or the push of a button.

Plastic or wicker boxes can be placed on lower shelves to store children's toys, video games, and the like. Bins and other containers can be used to gather video game controllers, game pieces and other equipment.

Family Room Clutter Busters

- Many clients will complain of general clutter always seeming to gather in their family rooms. You can suggest an "out-basket" of items that don't belong in the room, or even numerous out-baskets for each room (kitchen, laundry, etc.) or person in the household.

- Some clients will have months of stacked up newspapers and magazines at the beginning of a purge. Sturdy canvas bags can hold already-read magazines and newspapers, and will be easy to stash away or transfer to the recycling bin.

- An unused fireplace can be fitted with a small shelving unit to create more room for books in a small living room.

- To display art treasures or things of beauty, curio cabinets can be used. One benefit of glass-enclosed cabinetry is that it reduces the necessity for dusting small collectibles.

- Teach clients to not let the clutter build up by initiating a daily routine. Empty ashtrays if there are smokers in the house, put back items that belong in other rooms, put away items that belong in the family room.

3.5.5 Laundry Rooms

It is amazing how a family can amass laundry, even over a week. Having the right space set up and a workable, organized routine are the basics for making clients' laundry rooms places of efficiency, not aggravation.

The ultimate purpose of a laundry room is to get dirty clothes cleaned, dried, and put away. To achieve this purpose you have to work with clients to help them discover if the space they have is working for them, and how they can plan a space and a routine that eases this necessary task.

For many clients the biggest organizational challenge in a laundry room is really about processing. Help them work out a laundry schedule that keeps things moving and doesn't let big piles build up. Everything that isn't part of the existing equipment and supplies of the laundry room should be put away after doing laundry to reduce clutter.

Storing Dirty Laundry

Probably the most important storage issue in a laundry area is where to house the laundry before clients are ready to do a wash. Some clients may choose to keep unwashed laundry in hampers that are not actually in their laundry areas, but some will want to have a central storage area in the laundry room.

Hampers are the traditional laundry holders in households, and they come in a variety of functional styles you can match to your clients' needs. Stationary hampers can be left in bathrooms or bedroom closets. They can be multi-purpose like wooden bench hampers, or a basket in traditional wicker. Your clients will use their laundry baskets or a laundry bag to gather laundry from stationary receptacles. Depending on need, you might also suggest a variation on the traditional:

- Rolling hampers can be moved throughout the house to gather laundry

- Collapsible hampers can be stored away when not in use

- Multi-bin hampers can help clients make it easy for their families to sort clothes by washing category as they leave them to be washed

- Hanging hampers can be hung over doors or on hooks to collect laundry

You can browse styles of hampers and baskets for your clients at the website below, or in any department or home decor store.

- *Organize.com — Hampers and Baskets*
  http://www.organize.com/hampersbaskets.html

Staging

Clients will require staging areas where soiled clothing can be presorted into piles by how items should be washed, and adequate storage places for washing supplies.

Simple wall-mounted shelves are easy to install, and can be moved anywhere they are needed if the space gets reorganized. They can be purchased at any home supply or lumber store.

If clients have large enough rooms, counter spaces or even old tables can be used as a workspace. Some organizers use kitchen islands in laundry rooms to create space to work and adequate storage. For tinier spaces, a collapsible table can be used and hung on a door or wall rack when not in use. As another option, freestanding laundry centers are similar to closet organizers. They include strong shelving, and rods for items on hangers.

Drying Space

A laundry area with ample room to hang or place clothing that must drip-dry is very convenient. Retractable clotheslines can be used and then retracted as a functional space-saving device.

There are also metal drying racks available for use in tiny laundry areas that fold flat and can be easily placed alongside the washer or dryer when not in use. Wall mounted clothes drying racks are attached to the wall and can be pulled out when in use and pushed back after use to save space.

If space is limited, tub-drying racks allow clients to dry their delicate and drip-dry clothes in the bathtub.

- *Organize.com — Drying Racks*
  www.organize.com/fldrra.html

Folding, Ironing and Hanging

Again, adequate work room is necessary to fold clothes. Irons, ironing boards, and ironing board accessories should be placed to allow clients to move from one laundry task to another without leaving the area to gather supplies. Suggest to clients that keeping a sewing kit on hand in the laundry room will also make quick fixes more convenient.

Here are some additional tips:

- Ironing board racks can be purchased, including over-the-door ironing board holders with or without attached accessory racks, and wall-mounted ironing board racks.

- Wall-mounted and freestanding rods designed to hold clothes on hangers are made in every price range, and some collapse for easy storage.

3.5.6 Dining Rooms

Eating together in an organized and attractive space can be a relaxing and happy experience. Unfortunately, dining room tables often end up being used as haphazard storage for mail, books, purses, briefcases, newspapers, magazines, and homework projects. A dining room that is ready to use – with a table that is cleared off and decorative – will be easier to use, and used more frequently.

Lose the Clutter

The first step to getting clients' dining rooms ready for dinner is to purge the existing clutter that makes its way to their dining room tables. Sit with clients and determine what items find their way to their dining room tables that shouldn't. Look for ways to properly categorize and help them plan routines to remove those items to the proper areas in their homes.

The first thing you should do is make sure there is adequate entryway storage in clients' homes. Suggest attractive entryway pieces such as storage benches, key and coat racks, and other units which can temporarily house the daily clutter. A closed cupboard allows items to be temporarily housed without creating a disorderly look — and if it is large enough, briefcases, purses, and backpacks can all be stowed until they are needed the following day. A basket or slot near the door can house the mail until clients are ready to sort through and file it away.

Storage Solutions

The main storage needed in dining rooms is for dining equipment such as tablecloths and napkins, placemats and trivets, and the good silverware and china. Additionally, all of these pieces must be reachable. Consider the ease of use rule — if an item is used frequently, it should be easy to reach.

> TIP: Talk with your clients about how their dining rooms are used. If they entertain frequently they will need a different setup than if they only use the dining room for two holidays a year.

Buffets are a nice choice for storage of dining equipment because they are secure and usually roomy enough for large serving platters and other pieces. Most buffets have several pullout drawers and a series of cupboards, which are lined with shelves. Additional pullout drawers in a buffet can be used to store linen or paper napkins, candles, candleholders, and trivets.

A china cabinet is an excellent way to show off beautiful pieces of china. Some china is as pretty as art, and when tastefully arranged it can really add to the overall look of a dining room. Make sure that plates are placed securely and that china cabinet doors shut well and latch.

If clients have closet spaces adjacent to their dining room, suggest they store table leaves as well as any extra large platters and other equipment that won't fit into a buffet there. Closet storage is also good for centerpiece storage — store seasonal centerpieces in well-marked containers so they will be easy to identify.

Table linen can be a hassle if it requires hours of ironing every time it is going to be used. While this may be unavoidable with tablecloths, at least placemats can be stored flat, without folds to ensure they are ready for the table when they are needed. Placing a number of placemats in a stack and matching napkins on top of the placemats can maximize space. Linen napkins that have been pre-folded and ironed save a lot of time, too. To maximize space, clients should place placemats and napkins in large, clear lidded plastic containers and then the space on top or below the mats can be used to best advantage.

The walls of a dining room can provide extra storage, too. Suggest to clients who have large libraries that empty dining room wall space can accommodate shelving units. Shelves can display books and curios to make interesting dinnertime conversation pieces.

Preventing Breakage

Fragile plates and stemware should be placed on stationary shelves instead of drawers, the movement of which can lead to breakage. They may also be safer options than a china cabinet for precious items that could be damaged by earthquakes or jarring.

Here are some more tips for helping clients prevent breakage:

- Use drawer dividers for silver, or keep it in a silver chest designed to protect it. Silver bags help protect silver from tarnishing, but they won't prevent it completely.

- Consider using Styrofoam plate protectors or cloth plate protectors for long-term storage of plates and other fine china in a buffet.

- To prevent chipping, make sure not to stack different size plates in a haphazard manner.

- The most fragile pieces should be as low to the ground as possible in buffet storage. Don't place heavy pieces on top of other pieces, and don't overfill a shelf.

- Don't place items next to each other that could possibly tip and break. When in doubt, wrap the items in protective covering before placement. Stemware should be placed rim-side down.

You can look at some protective equipment at the following websites:

- *Plate Protectors*
www.shoestringacres.com/bardsprotectors.htm

- *Stacks and Stacks.com — Stemware Storage Chest*
www.stacksandstacks.com/html/10294_stemware-chest.htm

3.5.7 Home Offices or Dens

Clients have bills to pay, warranties to hold onto, and birth certificates to file. They will need a designated place in their homes in which they can organize all of this "business of life" and be able to easily find it again when they need it. Your clients will often tell you they have spent hours looking for something important, because they don't have systems to keep those everyday details in life from getting out of control.

Home office spaces or dens can also be more than just places to store personal papers. They can be virtual offices for those times that members of clients' households want to work at home, where their children might do Internet research for homework and reports, and to house clients' collectables and personal library.

Tell your clients that once a home office or den is organized, their efficiency goes up and their stress goes down. They may even have time to dust off and read one of those great books in their library!

Personal Records and Documents

The first step to getting clients' home offices or dens organized is to help them purge their personal records. Use these steps to sort through their personal records. Once the purge has taken place, you are ready to help clients store their information.

Purge the Easy Stuff

Duplicate copies of bills, junk mail, old magazines and newspapers, and any papers they no longer have any use for can all be shredded and recycled. Teach clients not to keep duplicate, out-dated, or damaged software, unneeded disks of old files or information (except for backup, of course). Other clutter culprits include old or unusable office supplies or broken equipment.

TIP: Identity theft is on the rise. Ensure clients shred all documents with family members' names, addresses, or any other vital information, including pre-addressed return envelopes from companies they do business with.

Purge Old Personal Records

How old is old? Here are some general retention rules — remember to adjust these to fit clients' special situations.

- *Bank records:* At least a year, sometimes permanently.

- *Bills:* At least a year, sometimes permanently.

- *Credit card receipts:* Two months to seven years.

- *Financial documents (e.g. IRA contributions, savings plans or retirement plan statements, and brokerage statements)*: Permanently, or, in the case of the brokerage statements, until the client sells their securities.

- *Mortgage information:* Six years, sometimes permanently.

- *Pay stubs:* One year.

- *Receipts:* One year; seven for items itemized on taxes.

- *Taxes:* Seven years.

- *Warranties:* Until the warranty runs out, or earlier if you no longer have the item.

These are guidelines only. Consult with further resources or a professional advisor on how long to keep specific records on hand. Bankrate.com has an article on "What Financial Records to Keep and How Long to Keep Them" at **www.bankrate.com/brm/news/pf/20060215b1.asp**.

Work Out a Filing System

Typical systems include alpha filing, numerical filing, and filing by date. You may use one system as a subset of another — for example, all bills filed alphabetically by the name of the billing company, and then each company's bills filed by date received. The important thing is that the system makes sense to the client. Online, an article titled "Learn how to Organize Bills" can be found at **http://arar.essortment.com/help payingbill_rire.htm**.

Storage Ideas

Home storage for personal documents can be simple or complex. Work with clients to see what method will work best for their personal styles and how they think. Once you have a system in mind, you may need to purchase office storage supplies such as:

- Filing cabinets

- Plastic filing boxes

- In-drawer file storage in desks

- Fire resistant strong boxes

- Bank safety deposit boxes

- File folders — legal size or letter size

- Hanging files

- Binders with plastic sheet covers

For the important or irreplaceable, suggest to clients that they have a safe, fire-resistant place (or better yet, a safe-deposit box) to keep birth certificates, wills, deeds, power of attorney, marriage, divorce and death certificates, and life insurance policies. Priceless family memorabilia should be stored in this manner, as should an inventory of household items for insurance purposes.

Many clients like to use their home office spaces to house their libraries, their collections and curios, and other memorabilia. These items are relatively simple to display and store. Storage ideas include bookcases, wall mounted-shelving units, and curio cabinets.

Books can be alphabetized by author. Some clients like to organize some sections by subject. Talk with clients about what works best for them. Collections and curios can be grouped into categories for a nice display. Memorabilia, depending on the items, can be housed in scrapbooks or displayed on shelves.

Layout and Setup

Many clients use their home office spaces for work or Internet time. Setup is important here to make sure equipment is conveniently placed, ready to be used, and that all necessary supplies are right where clients need them to be.

Ease of use and proximity rules will apply in home office or den setup. Just like in a family room, equipment must be plugged in, set up and ready to go. Supplies should be placed conveniently for ease of use in desks, or on shelving units.

> **TIP:** Consider using plastic silverware organizers in desk drawers for easy organizers for pens, pencils and other small home office supplies.

Some professional organizers say that the best way to create home office storage space is to transform a traditional closet into a shelved storage area — supplies are out of sight, and there is plenty of space.

3.5.8 Attics, Basements, and Garages

Attics don't have to be creepy and dusty like they are depicted in movies. Basements don't have to be burial grounds for broken appliances, and garages don't have to be neighborhood eyesores.

All of these spaces can be functional storage solutions that allow the rest of the house to run smoothly. Whether clients want to store camping equipment, high school memorabilia, out-of-season sporting equipment, or archived files, any of these spaces can work to make wonderful solutions for long-term storage.

Attics, basements, and even garages can also be transformed into living spaces, as offices, playrooms, workrooms or family rooms. The lack of definition in these spaces is what allows clients to use them creatively.

When working with clients to help them organize their attics, basements, and garages, make sure to discuss in depth their ultimate goals for each space. Do they want to create storage, or transform a space into extra living space — or both? Getting clear will allow you to make good suggestions based on knowing what they consider their "best-case scenario."

Evaluate the Space

Before you decide how to use any of these spaces, you'll need to ask the client some questions to determine if there are any limitations based on one of the following factors.

Is the Space Finished or Unfinished?

Unfinished spaces will lend themselves to storage but not much else, unless clients are hiring contractors. Finished spaces can be living spaces and storage spaces combined.

What Kind of Access is There?

Some attics are only accessible from tiny push-up hatches. If the only opening to an attic is miniscule, this will dramatically limit the storage opportunities. However, if the attic is accessible by a good-sized opening with a drop-down ladder, a retractable ladder, or even stairs, the possibilities increase.

How Much Space is Available?

Spaces have to be clear enough — too much insulation in an attic or plain old lack of space will make storage difficult.

Is There Any Lighting?

There must be light so clients can see what they are doing in their space.

Is Ventilation Sufficient?

Mechanical attic fans can be installed but they need to have an automatic shut-off feature if the temperature gets too hot, since they can cause fires if not installed properly. Insist that your clients have these installed by professionals.

Is There a Floor?

There has to be something to walk on. If there is no flooring, plywood flooring can be added, but again, a professional should add it.

Is it Warm and Clean Enough?

Unfinished spaces will be prone to more dust and changes in temperature. These should be considered when making storage plans. Use storage boxes that withstand changes in temperature and that are as airtight as possible to prevent dust from getting in.

Is it Dry Enough?

Basements can make excellent storage spaces providing they aren't overly damp. Even though houses are engineered today to try to prevent this, sometimes basements flood. Another problem with basement storage can be humidity, which can cause items to mildew. You can use metal shelving units that stand up off of the floor a bit, and/or a dehumidifier. Make sure to suggest tightly sealed plastic containers for stored items.

Long-Term Storage Items

Once you have evaluated whether or not the space can be used, help clients maximize it by purging the current or planned contents of these long-term storage areas. Make piles of Treasure, Trash, Tools and Toys, as explained earlier.

Then help clients determine the categories of stuff that remain and group them. The client might be looking to accommodate items such as:

- Christmas decorations

- Memorabilia

- Books

- Out-of-season clothing

- Gardening supplies

- Tools and a tool bench

- Craft and hobby supplies

- Sporting equipment

- Cleaning materials and supplies

- Automotive supplies

Make sure the client is not storing things they simply don't know what to do with. Suggest to your clients that they thoroughly examine all contents of boxes they plan to store and throw away or donate everything they can before proceeding.

Tell clients to also make routine checks of basements and attics to make sure that stored items are protected and in good condition.

Long-Term Storage Solutions

To maximize long-term storage space, use stackable plastic boxes. Don't stack the rows of storage too deeply to retrieve things, though.

Hang out-of-season clothing in protective zipper wardrobe bags to protect them from moisture and dust. These can be found in plastic or canvas as seen at **www.comforthouse.com/dressbagsetof2.html**.

Garage storage units are made to be installed into garages to enhance their storage capabilities. They include rafter-hanging shelves to create space for boxes; overhead storage hooks for bikes and other equipment; and wall-mounted racks for cleaning supplies, tools, gardening tools, and other supplies. You can see examples of products at **www. organizes-it.com/garage.php**.

HyLoft USA (**www.hyloftusa.com**) makes ceiling-mounted shelving units that come in a range of sizes and shapes. These shelves are wonderful storage for attics, basements or garages. They are easy to install and easy to purchase at a variety of home stores.

3.6 Organizing for Businesses

The process of organizing for businesses has five main components that are individual areas but that affect each other. Helping clients get their businesses in order may be a question of office setup, it may a case of simple clutter, or it may be that the amount of work they are trying to process isn't scheduled properly and they are falling behind.

In the following section you will learn how to help business clients organize their:

- Workspace

- Paper information

- Digital information

- Workflow design

- Project management

3.6.1 Assessing the Need

"When I do a consultation I say to the client, 'Tell me what you need, tell me where the pain is, and tell me what I can do to help improve this situation.' And then we start talking about steps to take."

— Ramona Creel, Professional Organizer

Some clients have labor-saving or convenient things right at their fingertips and yet they are so overwhelmed with work that they forget to use them. Or, because they are busy they don't bother to get things organized and set up how they want them, then they spend all day being frustrated but still feeling like they don't have time to rectify the situation.

Workplace Organizational Assessment

KEY: **A** = Always

                U = Usually

                S = Sometimes

                R = Rarely

1. I can find whatever I need on my desk.   A U S R

2. I am on time for meetings.   A U S R

3. I feel confident about my work.   A U S R

4. I never miss deadlines.   A U S R

5. I know where my last employee review is.   A U S R

6. I can locate copies of my last three paychecks.   A U S R

7. I back up my computer files weekly.   A U S R

8. I feel happy and calm at work.   A U S R

9. I don't have to work overtime to complete regular work.   A U S R

10. I file weekly.   A U S R

11. My coworkers feel like they can count on me.   A U S R

12. I know how each project I am involved in is doing.   A U S R

13. I do my share of the work on projects.   A U S R

14. I am asked to lead groups or be in other positions of responsibility.   A U S R

15. Coworkers seek out my opinions.   A U S R

16. I reply to my email promptly.   A U S R

17. I respond to my phone messages daily.   A U S R

18. I enjoy working with my coworkers.   A U S R

19. The last group project I completed was successful.   A U S R

20. There is a fair division of work on team projects.   A U S R

Let your clients know that no matter how busy they are, how pushed they are to make deadlines, or how behind they are at work — they must take the time to get things in order or the situation will not improve.

In many business situations there are obstacles that add to their disorganization problems. These can include:

- Not having access to organizing supplies

- Working for a disorganized person

- Having disorganized coworkers

- Lack of communication with the work group

- Too much workload

- Poor scheduling of work

Sometimes clients will only be able to actively control their individual issues. They may have a disorganized boss who will not stop overbooking his or her schedule; or they may have unrealistic workflow that is impossible to change.

While you can help clients pinpoint those things that are out of their control and discuss with them possible team communication options, they can't always solve problems with teammates. What you can do is help them discover strategies to help them work with unavoidable organizational problems and come up with best responses that will work for them.

You can use the assessment on page 113 to help clients analyze organizational issues in the workplace. The assessment covers organizational issues for the individual (first 10 questions), as well as how they function as part of a team (last 10 questions).

The assessment can be used to evaluate the organization as a whole, or it can be broken down into individual/group issues. The more "always" or "usually" answers there are in total for each section, the better that area of work is functioning. If you notice that there are many "sometimes" or "rarely" answers, this indicates an area of organization that you may wish to evaluate for change.

Business Consideration Form

You can use this business consideration form to help your clients hone in on their project organizational needs.

Client's name: _____

Company: _____

Address: _____

_____

Telephone: _____

Email: _____

Workspace
Describe the client's workspace issues:

_____

_____

_____

_____

Data
Describe the client's data issues:

_____

_____

_____

_____

Workflow
Describe the client's workflow issues:

_____

_____

_____

_____

Project Management
Describe the client's project management issues:

_____

_____

_____

_____

_____

Additional Notes:

_____

_____

_____

_____

_____

3.6.2 Workspace and Equipment

Clients in organized business environments are simply more productive. To find out how to help clients with their workspaces you need to ask:

- What is wrong with the space now?

- What are the most frustrating things that are happening or not happening?

- What is not getting accomplished that should be?

- What isn't easy to use?

- What can't they find?

- What would their ultimate office space look like?

- What are they trying to accomplish?

- What is their daily and weekly schedule?

Getting a workspace in order begins with taking a look at the actual space and its contents. Does the client have everything he or she needs to get their work done? Do they waste time searching for things they can't find? Are they working in a comfortable, appealing space? This section gives you some tips to help clients with these issues.

Space Setup

Office setup and productivity have a lot to do with one another. Workspace and equipment need to be used efficiently. Make sure clients use all equipment and furniture to their best advantage. In an ideal world we would all have unlimited space to set up our equipment and get organized, but the truth is that most workspaces are rather small. If clients are in cubicles, the space is even more limited.

Clients should make the time to properly set up available helpful supplies, furniture or other equipment, and correct broken equipment problems. A good floor plan design will help clients to use the space they have to best advantage. Talk with your clients about their current floor plans in relationship to the problems that they are having in their spaces.

The Desk

The desk in a workspace is the item that the rest of a floor plan revolves around, so make sure it is easy to access. Clients should have the most useful and comfortable desk possible. Make sure desk spaces are clear enough for use, with adequate room for monitors, keyboards and mouse pads. Desk drawers must be purged of the unnecessary, and then reorganized on the principles of proximity and ease of use.

Additional Workspace

Depending on the type of work they do, clients may need to have additional workspace that remains uncluttered and ready to use. Sometimes extra tables can provide these workspaces; sometimes credenzas or horizontal file cabinet tops will be the right height for workspaces. Make sure that the workspace doesn't become another catchall for clutter, and that it is conveniently placed near enough for the client to use it with ease.

The Computer and Peripherals

Make sure computers are stored in a way that is easy for clients to reach them to change CDs or disks, but that are not in the way. Ideally clients will be able to get to the back of units to change peripheral cords easily, or have front access for these items.

Peripheral equipment like printers, scanners, external modems, high speed Internet connection equipment and digital cameras should all be placed out of direct work-spaces but still close enough to access easily. Clients should not have to get up to get something from the printer if they use their printers all day long. The cords for computers and peripherals should be plugged into surge bars and neatly wound and tied to prevent tripping and fire hazards.

Filing Cabinets

Filing cabinets are absolutely necessary for clients to keep clutter off their desks and out of their workspaces. Make sure filing cabinets are well positioned and secured for safety. One client a professional organizer worked with had a filing cabinet that her colleagues laughingly called "the death trap." Filing cabinets should also be in good repair. Rollers need to be working well, and metal rods to hold hanging files need to be aligned. If they need to be locked, the keys should be in a safe but easy-to-access location.

Ergonomics

In the office, "ergonomics" means ensuring the elements of the work-space fit the individual person, instead of the person trying to fit into the space. This means that all furniture and equipment should be the right size, and allow the client to have a comfortable range of motion. Everything needs to fit the people using them in a healthy way.

If clients' space doesn't fit them, eventually it will become unhealthy. It is helpful for you to have a basic understanding of ergonomics and how you can help clients set up their spaces to have ergonomic features:

- Make sure that the furniture fits the clients, and that the computer equipment is placed to allow for best range of motion, height and reach.

- Clients should have wrist pads for use with their mouse pads and keyboards.

- Clients should have the very best and most comfortable chairs that you can dig up. Suggest that the client invest in a good chair with lumbar support, even if they have to buy it and bring it to work.

- Clients should have adequate room for their legs (it's amazing how many people store things under their desks).

- Check that computer monitors are at the proper height on desks for clients' ease of use and comfort. Monitors at improper heights can increase eyestrain and glare, and contribute to back and neck pain.

To learn more about ergonomics and its relation to your business clients, you can follow these links:

- *CergoS – What is Ergonomics?*
  www.orosha.org/cergos/ergo.html

- *Ergonomics for Beginners*
  www.micronite.com/html/books/0748408258.htm

Emotional Appeal

Clients need to feel like their workspace is an emotionally healthy place for them to be. Studies have proven that people who are genuinely comfortable in their workspace and feel good in it have dramatically increased work performance.

This is a matter of personal preference for clients, but there are some standard things that you can suggest, including:

- Plants

- Artwork

- Family photos

- Music

- A tabletop fountain

- A mirror

- Awards or motivational pieces

Don't forget the fun stuff, too — something that reminds clients that they have a life outside work. For example, one organizer's client really enjoyed a talking "Dr. Evil" figurine that offered pithy sayings whenever he needed a think-break. Just make sure there are not so many personal things that the person becomes distracted or overwhelmed by clutter.

3.6.3 The "Paper Trail"

Sometimes the main organizational problem in a workspace is that the client seems to have "lost" his or her desk. It's probably under there somewhere, but the client has given up the hope of ever seeing it again!

Most people in offices don't enjoy filing, so they allow piles and piles of papers to gather before ever giving them a thought. One professional organizer had a client who said that he usually hired a temp once a month to do his filing, and meanwhile just threw everything on a table. While that is definitely a "system" – he hires someone to dig him out – it's not a great situation in between visits from the temp.

Paper can be overwhelming in an office. Not only can disorganized papers be stressful, but in a business environment disorganization can mean missed deadlines, missed appointments and meetings, and poor work quality. All of this causes workplace stress. And if work is stressful, it just isn't any fun to be there.

The Importance of Filing

File organization is very important for two reasons. Long-term files are the memory banks of the company, and short-term files are primary tools in clients' everyday workflow.

Employees, even the owners, come and go, but the files are forever. Files contain the company's trade secrets and intellectual property. The information in the files can defend a company in a lawsuit. Clients' files hold their customer lists and even some secrets of their customers. Critical financial information and transaction histories with customers and suppliers are all sitting in the files.

Some filing is also done to support everyday workflow. Some of the materials used in these processes are created for temporary use and will not be retained permanently — but they are needed in the short term to get a job done.

A Good Filing System

So, what makes a good filing system? It's one that the client will use. Storage of records should be easy to do, and the search and retrieval of records should come easily even to those unfamiliar with the system. The best way to ensure that clients file is to create systems that make it as easy as possible. Here are some tips to use:

- The arrangement of the files should support the processes of the file users. As appropriate, file alpha-numerically by subject or category, or chronologically by date.

- An information map showing the layout of the files and the logical relationships between the sections should be plainly displayed.

- Use visual helpers, such as color-coded files and well-labeled cabinets. Special-handling files (sensitive, urgent) are clearly identifiable.

- Unnecessary information should not be stored. Active files should be routinely purged and inactive files archived to long-term storage. "To-be filed" stacks are frequently cleared out.

- In larger offices, files taken out of the cabinets are marked by a card letting other users know who has the record.

- For large files, break the file down into more manageable sections. A helpful product is the six-section classification folio that is a multi-section file folder with brad-type fasteners to hold documents in place.

A Clearly Defined Retention Policy

When you see signs that clients are keeping everything, coach them on keeping what is necessary and have them destroy the rest. Section 3.5.7 has tips and advice for what should be kept and for how long, but businesses should also have situation-specific rules, and rules governing internal communication.

A records retention policy should be put in place so that all employees are familiar with what is to be kept and what is to be destroyed. A good records retention policy will contain:

- A clear definition of a retainable record

- A clear definition of destroyable working materials

- A records retention schedule (how long certain things must be maintained)

- Storage rules

- Records retirement and disposition

- Disaster preparedness and recovery

- Policies to protect sensitive information

TIP: Some contracts may also require that the client retain certain records for a period of time.

Things to Avoid

There are typical pitfalls businesses fall into. Remind your client to be wary of:

- Allowing a "to-be-filed" stack of folders to pile up

- Keeping materials past their need date

- Keeping files "just in case"

- Failing to review and purge on a regular basis

- Filing duplicate materials

- Not communicating filing procedure to all employees

3.6.4 Digital Information

Digital business records are as important to a business as paper records are. Business information has to be well organized or the business is in trouble, and digital data is subject to the same legal and contractual retention requirements as paper records, so your clients will need a system for filing data.

In addition to the documents they work with, it is common for clients to get hundreds of pieces of email every week. Increasingly, unwanted junk email, called "spam," is cluttering electronic mailboxes and taking clients' time away from productive tasks. It's easy to see how clients can get stressed out and overwhelmed.

The primary areas for digital information organization and management are:

- Computer files and organization

- Email

- Databases

Computer Files

Now that every computer has hard drives with huge amounts of space to store files, the number of files has grown to fill the new limit. Clients can't find the files that they know are on their machine somewhere. Here are a few techniques to keep personal computer files organized.

Segregate Temporary from Permanent

Clients should segregate their permanent files from the temporary files.

- Temporary files should be deleted when the work is complete and the final report has been moved into the permanent file area.

- Permanent files not likely to be needed again in the next six months should be archived on a CD or other storage medium.

Use Naming Conventions

When there are lots of files and folders to search and sort through, a good folder and file naming convention will simplify clients' lives. The details of the naming preferences are not as important as that a convention is used consistently. The main point of naming conventions is ease of retrieval later on.

Use dates in folder or file names where it makes sense, and be as descriptive as possible when selecting a name. Use keywords in the name that are common search terms. Here's a sample convention for filing invoices. All files contain the code INV, which is a term that can be searched.

FILE NAME:	Invoices (INV) 2007
SUBFOLDERS:	INV January 2007, INV February 2007, INV March 2007, etc.
INVOICES:	INV-JAN 15/07; INV-JAN 31/07; INV-FEB 15/07

Use Folder Trees and Hierarchies

Clients should create a file structure on the computer that makes it fast and easy to find the files they need. When a folder tree is making it harder to find what clients need, evaluate whether the hierarchy is too cumbersome, has too much old data, or has inconsistent naming practices. Encourage clients to throw out structures that do not work and start over again. Here are some additional tips:

- Limit the number of files in each folder to 50

- Group folders into logical collections with other folders

- Avoid too many "layers" of subfolders

- Avoid using the same name or very similar names for different folders

- For image files, use "thumbnail" view mode to see mini-versions of the contents

Use Shared Files

Many businesses use shared file directories on the company network. Many people in a workgroup can access a large number of files without having a personal copy. If clients' businesses are suffering from too many people with different versions of the same file, or too many people are hanging onto personal copies of the same file, encourage those clients to consider shared file servers for this purpose.

Advanced Search and Indexing

If all these safeguards are in place and a file still gets lost, a way to speed up the search and retrieval process is to use advanced search functions. Some of the ways that a search can be constructed include:

- Search by date

- Search by file type (e.g., Word, PowerPoint, etc.)

- Search by file size

Digital Organizing Tools

Clients may have calendars that they use at home, others on their desktop computers, and perhaps others on their handheld organizers.

As mentioned earlier in this guide, having more than one primary calendar is an easy way to lose track of appointments and to-do lists. No matter what type suits clients best, encourage them to stick with only one primary calendar. The client may have to coordinate their primary calendar with calendars used by the rest of the family at home or the rest of the workgroup.

Email

Many of your clients will have more incoming email than they can handle, and no system for organizing the messages. Their inbox may be bursting with hundreds of emails (many unread) and they will not know they are missing key communication.

Other clients keep everything "just in case," but when "just in case" occurs, they don't know how to find the message they needed. Some clients hang onto old email because they might want to contact the sender again someday. These clients are simply forgetting to use the address book/personal contacts function.

The first step in getting control of email is to analyze how and why your client uses it. Then you'll be ready to help them develop a system for this fast and furious method of communication. Here are some tips you can offer your clients.

Managing your Inbox

Process each message as it comes in: read, reply or forward, and then file or delete. If the email contains an attached file that merits keeping, they should save the attachment and delete the email. For email that clients do not want to delete, first suggest they decide if the email is being kept permanently or temporarily. Remind clients that email is never a place for long-term storage or formal records retention.

Choosing the Right Storage Method

For messages that clients are temporarily not ready to delete, move them out of the active inbox and into offline email temporary storage. If the email software the client uses has a task manager, then they can drag and drop the message into the task area. Emails can then be deleted because the task utility will store the message.

The task function will let clients set dates to remind them to open the tasks and take appropriate action on those dates, and can be further classified by priority. Clients will then have clear, prioritized to-do lists built right into their email environments. Deadlines embedded in email can also transfer to the calendar reminder function.

> **TIP:** If messages should be kept permanently, save them and the attachments to the computer hard drive and file and retain the records according to company policies.

Avoiding Unwanted Email

Make sure your clients use spam-filtering software. Additionally, most email software has built-in programs called rules or macros that can help your clients sort their mail and delete junk before they see it.

Keeping "Sent" Mail

There are certainly reasons to keep copies of email messages that clients have sent themselves. The rules for retaining or destroying these messages are no different than for messages they received. Hang on to anything needed while the work associated with it is still in process. But when the work is finished, retain permanent records according to company policy and destroy temporary work products.

Purging All Email Files Regularly

The most important way to clear through the clutter is to purge! Teach clients to be ruthless with deleting email that they no longer need to respond to. If the message contains a formal record that should be kept as part of the company's records retention policy, then save the message outside of the email utility and archive it electronically, on CD, or paper.

Organizing Databases

A database is an organized collection of information. Databases drive most of the information used in business processes today. A company's performance and reputation can ride on the integrity and effectiveness of a database, so when a database has organizational problems, then the business has real trouble on their hands.

While your clients should understand that you are not a computer programmer or engineer, a professional organizer can help a client with both data integrity (the quality of the data), and make suggestions for the organizational design of the database based on the principles explained in this section. The main things that can affect data integrity are accuracy, currency, and consistency.

Ensuring Data Accuracy

When data is collected and entered by hand, people make mistakes. To help ensure data accuracy:

- Focus on making sure the data is good before it enters the database

- When possible, don't retype information — use electronic data from an original source

- Do random spot-checks of data entered

- Only enter the minimum information needed

- Configure data entry screens to prevent common errors

- Ensure data entry clerks get plenty of mental and physical breaks

- Check the data for accuracy using regularly scheduled audits

- When errors are found, look for trends to catch more of the same

Ensuring Data Currency

Data should be as up to date as possible. To help ensure data currency:

- Use automatic-update data feeds as much as possible

- Update as frequently as you can get changes

- Automatically purge old data

- Hold off major business events until the database is ready to reflect the new data

Ensuring Data Consistency

Data consistency is a company-wide agreement to store two similar pieces of information in the database the same way.

To help ensure data consistency:

- Use standard spellings and definitions

- Use standards of classification

- Agree to common units of measure

- Make sure everyone who can enter information is familiar with database protocol

Technology Tips from an Expert

"I read once that if you know only 10% of everything there is to know about the computer world you can be called an expert. I may know seven or eight percent. I tell my clients upfront about things that I don't know. When I have computer issues that I don't know the answer to, I call in an expert myself."
— Rozanne Hird, Professional Organizer

Professional organizer Rozanne Hird's specialty is technology. Rozanne works with home office, small office, and corporate clients helping them organize their technology. She shared the following tips for helping professional organizers help their clients with technology.

1. Clear the Desktop. Many clients have all kinds of icons on their computer's desktop, many for things they don't use at all. They are afraid to delete anything, because they may not know what it is, or believe that deleting the shortcut would delete the program. Cleaning up the desktop is a great first step to digital organization.

2. Use a Temporary Folder. When clients don't know exactly what do to with a document they have just created or downloaded, suggest they create a "Temporary" folder within their "My Documents" folder. Clients should schedule a time to review, organize and/or delete the contents as necessary.

3. Back Up Data. Clients should be told to back up files weekly as a minimum. If the data is of a critical nature, clients should back up even more frequently. If clients put all the things they create, download, and receive through email into their "My Documents" folder and create subfolders under that, then there is only one folder to back up, which both shortens and simplifies the process. Also, have rotating backup media. Don't use just one CD, zip drive disk, floppy disk, etc., in case there is a flaw in the media.

4. Protection from Viruses. Encourage your clients to get good virus software. A virus can easily destroy data, and when virus software packages start at $50-$75, it isn't worth taking a risk.

One last piece of advice: Carry a screwdriver set for minor repairs that clients have with their hardware!

3.6.5 Organizing Workflow

In business, products must be created or services performed in the most efficient and cost-effective manner possible. The steps used to create products or perform services are called processes or workflow. The steps to designing a good workflow are identifying waste, focusing on value creation, and getting everyone in the process involved.

To begin, have your clients explain the workflow to you, using flowcharts if necessary. When one or more of the following clues are present, there is usually a good opportunity to help clients improve workflow and increase efficiency and profits:

- The time to complete a process varies

- Excess inventories, rework, or scrap are common

- Work sits in queues waiting for the next step in the process to happen

- Customers are dissatisfied with the quality of the products or services

- Employees or supervisors cannot accurately explain the entire process

- Employees and equipment are idle, waiting for work to arrive

- Employees don't follow the formal written processes

Identify Waste

Waste isn't always something clients can see — it can also take the form of wasted time or wasted money. Anything that does not add value to the creation or delivery of product or services should be considered waste. Look to eliminate the following types of waste:

Defects

Look at processes to discover the root causes of defects. If a process creates defective results, using an inspection at the end of the process to catch defects rarely makes the process any better. What kinds of defects are causing scrap or rework? If clients cite multiple reasons for the defects, then take them on one at a time until the problem is resolved. Recommend that clients conduct in-process inspections to catch problems before they move on down the line.

Lost Time

Inactive people or equipment is a cost that is not contributing to profits or the process of making products. Help clients determine if workers or equipment can be used to perform more than one function. Another form of wasted waiting is for a product or service to sit in a queue waiting to get worked on. Are some people or equipment overbooked and causing backups in the workflow?

Excess Transporting

Look for ways to minimize the number of times, or the amount of time, spent moving products or people. If some work has to be done in one place and the next step in the process has to be done in another place, the time and cost to move the product to the next station can be costly.

Excess Inventory

Search stock rooms with old parts or materials that have been lying around unused for a long time. These items are company "assets," but are not contributing to production, service, or the profits of the business.

Excess Processing

Help clients stick to steps that deliver only what their customers want. Identify this type of waste by looking at each step in the workflow and asking, "Why does the customer want this done?" Sometimes processes may be done out of habit and don't make any difference in the end product.

Lack of Communication

You may discover that two employees are doing the same task, unbeknownst to each other. Your client can save time and resources by making sure that all employees have a defined role and a manual that explains their responsibilities. Weekly meetings can help make sure that everyone who needs to be is in the know on new projects.

Overly Complex

It is easy for processes to evolve over time and turn into something never intended. Are your clients doing something the hard way? Ask yourself the following questions as you review the workflow:

- Can everyone involved easily explain each process step simply?

- Are workflow charts confusing?

- Do processes seem overwhelmed by bureaucracy?

Inappropriate Inventory Levels

When clients can't fill orders fast enough, customers have to wait for the product, driving down their level of satisfaction, causing them to consider the competition next time. When clients build up stockpiles of finished products, they are spending money making products no one is paying for. Even worse, having finished inventory on-hand can cause clients to pay higher taxes. Help clients look for ways to predict demand and scale production accordingly.

Focus on Value Creation

Any steps in the workflow that do not satisfy the customer, ensure excellent quality, or transform the product in a way that brings it closer to completion are not creating value for your clients' businesses. Look for the following when evaluating processes:

A Streamlined Process of Transformation

Whether the process is turning a tree into a table or turning information into reports, an organized workflow focuses on moving the product closer to the final form and getting it in the hands of customers. Examples of process steps that don't transform the product are inspecting, sorting, warehousing, and transporting. A lean, streamlined workflow minimizes any of these steps that don't add something to the product.

A Product That Meets (Not Exceeds) Requirements

Help your clients to determine what their customers really want to pay for, and what processes are expendable. Have your clients take a look at the difference between their products or services and their competitors. This is another way to determine what customers are willing to pay extra for and what can be cut out. Remember to help clients to build in acceptable quality in every step of the process.

Standardized Workflow

As an outsider to the business operations, a professional organizer can often help identify where steps in the workflow are inconsistent or change according to a variety of conditions. When all the steps in the workflow are broken down into standard, repeatable work functions and packages, clients have a baseline upon which to define the workflow and evaluate suggestions for improvement. Standard work is easier to measure, teach, inspect, plan, and resource.

Measurable Progress

Many times clients will be frustrated with a process, but they haven't taken the time to measure how well the process is working. Get clients to agree to a set of measurements that show the workers how well they are performing to management's goals (make sure the measurements reflect the right goals).

Get Everyone Involved

The best people to talk to about where the problems are in a workflow are the workers who deal with it on a daily basis. The workers who perform the process can make it very easy or very hard to make changes stick. Here are some ways to help clients get everyone involved in workflow processes to be a committed part of the team.

Employee Involvement

Clients should put one or two workers on the workflow improvement team. When they participate in the decision-making, they will give the new changes their best efforts at helping it succeed. Note that when union workers are involved in the process, changes in job duties and job descriptions are often controlled by the collective bargaining agreement, so make sure changes are coordinated with the union representation.

Rewards and Recognitions

Be sure your clients thank and reward everyone with some sort of celebration when the changes take effect and the results prove the benefits. It doesn't have to be something too expensive, but might involve pictures of the team on the wall with a paragraph of thanks and a description of their accomplishments; an article in the company newsletter; a team party in the lunchroom, or certificates of achievement delivered personally by senior management.

Short-Term Victories

When a workflow organization project is very big and complex it can take a long time to see the changes take effect. Remember that the right way to eat an elephant is one bite at a time! Suggest to clients that when planning the work, they build intermediate steps that show progress and proof of the value of the proposed changes. Clients should schedule status reports to keep everyone posted on progress, and post progress charts or models where everyone can see them.

3.6.6 Project Management

A project is a planned activity, usually involving several steps or tasks, the goal of which is to accomplish some tangible and definite result. A project has a beginning and an end.

A professional organizer may act as both a troubleshooter and a consultant in helping clients take a look at their existing projects and identifying ways that they can organize projects more efficiently. Certainly, you are not expected to be an expert in a company's area of business or expertise, but good project organization skills are necessary to keep plans on budget, on time, and on track to deliver the desired results.

In a small company, you may help the owner organizing a project one-on-one. In a larger company, you may work with an onsite project manager, overseeing a project with hundreds of team members. In some companies you might even be asked to help project teams learn of the organizational steps of successful project management.

The components of good project organization are:

- *Planning the Project:* The most important part of a successful project is the planning phase — figuring out what will happen when, and how much it will cost.

- *Monitoring Performance:* Once the effort begins, clients need to monitor their performance and keep track of their progress.

- *Risk Management:* To minimize the impact of uncertainty, special attention must be constantly given to potential risks.

- *Customer Involvement:* Clients' customers need to be members of the team so they can be in the loop — they need to be a part of key decisions that are made during the course of the project so that they will be satisfied with the end result.

Projects You May Encounter

Your clients will have projects of every size and scope. Imagine that...

...a food bank needs to find and move into a larger facility

...a charity wants to conduct a major fund-raising event

...a company wants to implement new inventory management software

All projects have some things in common. Clients will have a limited amount of money to spend; they will need the job done in a certain time frame; and they will have an expectation of what a successful outcome for the project should be.

In a business environment, a project can be externally or internally focused. The first is a project to generate profits. The end result of this sort of project is something that is created and delivered to a customer. The second kind of project is done for the company itself — either an individual or a department inside a company.

Key 1: Planning the Project

The most important part of project organization and management happens in the planning stage — before any of the real work begins. Although clients will be anxious to get started, your best service to them will be to make sure they complete all of the planning activities needed before they begin.

Define the Project

Suggest to clients that getting things in writing, samples, pictures, and models are all good ways to begin. If there are known budget or time limits they need to be spelled out, and most importantly, everyone should be clear on the final objective.

Set Some Limits

Aspects of a project might not be affordable, might be too complicated, or may take a long time. Find out which things on this list are "must haves" and which are "nice to haves."

Evaluate and Account for Risk

Most clients tend to create plans that assume that everything is going to work out perfectly the first time. Expect some problems to occur. More information about risk management is provided further on in this section.

Determine Resources

Projects will require resources: a place to happen, probably some equipment, maybe some materials, and certainly some people to do the work. These things are called resources and without them, clients' projects can't get done. Have clients create detailed resource lists for each task in the project. Failure to check and balance resources is a reason that clients get surprised and fall into disorganization.

Set a Budget

You can use the project planning tools in this section to estimate costs, based on the resources needed, and how long they are needed for.

The Action Plan

One you have all the details, make an action plan that has a task-by-task breakdown of the project. The facing page shows a sample *Action Plan Task Worksheet*.

Key 2: Monitoring Performance

When the planning stops and the project begins, the organizer's job now becomes one of measurement, status, and decision support. Work with your clients to create and follow a plan to regularly review progress against schedule, cost, final outcome, and risk. A disciplined approach to project management will keep things from falling through the cracks. The questions clients will be asking every morning are:

- Is the project plan working?

- Is the project on schedule?

- Is the project on budget?

Is the Project Plan Working?

You will help organize clients' ongoing project data gathering and reporting process. Any technical issues or concerns that might impact the final product or project cost or schedule should be monitored and reported to project management. Be sure to help clients to present the information in a digestible form — with too much data, they lose focus on the most critical items.

Action Plan Task Worksheet

Task Description:

_____

_____

Person(s) to Complete Task:

Name	Hours	Cost	Qualifications or training needed?
_____	____	____	_____
_____	____	____	_____
_____	____	____	_____
_____	____	____	_____

Materials Needed:

Description	Amount	Cost
_____	_____	_____
_____	_____	_____
_____	_____	_____
_____	_____	_____

Equipment Needed:

Description	Amount	Cost
_____	_____	_____
_____	_____	_____
_____	_____	_____
_____	_____	_____

Facilities Needed:

Description	Amount	Cost
_____	_____	_____
_____	_____	_____
_____	_____	_____
_____	_____	_____

Start Date: _____   **End Date:** _____

Estimated Time to Complete: _____

Total Estimated Cost: _____

Is the Project on Schedule?

Clients need to monitor if their project is on schedule. The project team should be reporting progress in regular intervals — at least weekly or bi-weekly. A standard method of reporting progress is to address every line item on a schedule (such as a Gantt schedule) with a simple status of percent completed. When the task is 40% complete at the halfway point, then the task is behind schedule. When a task is 75% complete at the halfway point, then the task is ahead of schedule.

Is the Project on Budget?

Clients need to understand what the rate of spending is expected to be, and then compare how actual spending has occurred. Knowing how well a project is doing on budget performance is more complicated than checking the daily bank balance, as there may be costs that don't appear there. Clients should be monitoring the plan against the real performance, and getting explanations for the differences.

Signs of Project Trouble

Clients' project dilemmas usually related to time, money, and/or the expected final result. You will see one or more of the following when a project is in trouble:

- Deadlines missed or delayed (time)

- Costs higher than expected (money)

- The project keeps getting bigger (expected results)

Delays are a sure sign that a project has gone off track. Project managers call this "slipping the schedule to the right." Schedule delays cost money or lost customer confidence. You will need to find out the reason for the delay. Did the project planning fail to predict a problem that came up? Did the team underestimate the difficulty of the tasks?

Costs getting out of hand are usually a result of poor planning. Project teams tend to be overly optimistic on the actual costs and typically fail to plan for any bumps in the road.

Project Planning Tools

The reason many clients need your help managing their project is that they try to do too much in their heads and lose track of priorities. You can help them by making sure they really do a thorough job of project planning that will carry them through all the way to the end. Visual tools such as the following are often helpful to clients with other things on their minds.

The PERT Chart

When the interaction and steps involved to complete a project are complex and time-sensitive, a simple flow chart just won't do the trick. PERT charts are visual planning tools that are useful for projects that demand coordination from numerous contractors, departments, or organizations. The PERT chart is used to develop schedules and identify all costs. To get an idea of how they look and work you can see a sample PERT chart coordinating a film production online at **www.smartdraw.com/examples/pert/ film_production.htm**

The Gantt Chart

Gantt charts are used to coordinate project schedules. A Gantt chart is a graph with a timeline across the bottom (or top) and a list of activities stacked on top of each other on the left. Activities and milestones are mapped into a calendar timeline so it is clear what activities need to happen first, what elements overlap, and what the start and finish ranges are for each contributor to a project. You can see a sample online and learn the basics of making a Gantt chart at the following websites:

- *Sample Gantt Chart – Project Development*
  www.smartdraw.com/tutorials/gantt/tutorial1.htm

- *Learn the Basic Concepts of Drawing a Gantt Chart*
  www.smartdraw.com/resources/centers/gantt/ tutorial1.htm

Many popular and affordable project management software packages can create PERT charts, Gantt charts, and perform other functions such as resource balancing. Most of these packages, such as Microsoft Office Project, are affordable and easy to use.

When the job keeps getting bigger, project teams are "shooting at moving targets," and the job never gets done. In project planning this is called "poor requirements definition."

Addressing Change

A major reason projects have trouble is because people keep adding to, or changing, the final vision. Change makes project management difficult. It affects cost (especially if materials have already been ordered) and it affects schedule (especially if some work has to be undone, redone, or if new resources are not available). If your clients' customers want a change in a project, there should be a formal agreement to change, with corresponding adjustments in cost and schedule. Clients' customers will often back down from unnecessary changes in this case.

Key 3: Managing Risk

Unexpected events happen. Plans fall apart. As a professional organizer, you can help clients anticipate uncertainty and manage project risks.

Using brainstorming techniques, clients should list all the things that can happen which will interrupt their plans. They can use their list of resources and their PERT charts as idea generators.

Next, clients need to prioritize this list. Note that anything that is not merely a possibility, but is already a fact or certainty, should be built into the existing project plans. They should also disregard anything that is obviously terribly remote (e.g., a hurricane in a landlocked location). If the chances of the event occurring are statistically insignificant, then don't waste time with it.

Clients should take their remaining risks and rate each of them on a simple two-level scale of high likelihood or low likelihood, as well as the severity of the impact if it does occur: very serious or considerably serious. Disregard risks that do not have a serious impact, even if they are likely.

Risk information can be presented visually using a *Certainty and Crisis Chart*. Have clients take each project risk and write it in the square that corresponds to the ratings they assigned. This chart will allow clients to address risks that are serious and certain first. The chart looks like this:

Certainty and Crisis Chart

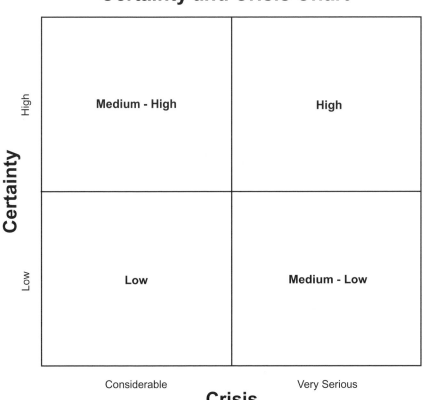

In most cases, with enough warning, clients can take action to avoid or prevent the crisis from happening, or at least to soften the impact if it does occur.

For every risk on their list, clients should develop a risk mitigation plan, which identifies actions that should be taken to avoid a risk or lessen its impact. These plans should be built into the project schedule. Deciding on the best risk mitigation strategy may not be simple, so use brainstorming techniques to generate a lot of different ideas. Clients should also schedule a review of the status of risks and their mitigation plans on a regular basis.

Project Risk Mitigation Worksheet

Risk Title: _____   Origin Date: _____

Risk Tracking No.: _____   Risk Level: _____

Risk Owner: _____

Risk Description:

_____

_____

Statement of Root Cause:

_____

_____

Impact if Risk is Realized (Plan, Schedule, Cost):

_____

_____

Mitigation Strategy:

❏ Avoid   ❏ Assume

❏ Transfer   ❏ Prevent/Control

Closure Criteria:

_____

_____

Fallback Alternatives:

_____

_____

Risk Level if Successful: _____

Is a Mitigation Action Plan Schedule With Resources Identified
Incorporated in the Project Schedule?   ❏ Yes   ❏ No

Last Date Risk Reviewed: _____

Date Closed Out: _____

Closed Out By: _____

Key 4: Customer Involvement

It is important to keep the voice of the "customer" heard on the project team, whether the customer exists, is internal, or is a projected target. If the customer cannot be present, then appoint someone on the team to act as the customer advocate during meetings and project reviews.

At key milestones in the project development, clients should schedule customer reviews where teams report on technical issues, schedule progress, and cost performance. Clients should discuss project risks and mitigation plans with their customers.

Many clients are surprised at how much their customers appreciate being treated like a member of the team and how helpful they can be. In the end, this type of engagement will build a strong working relationship with the customer who will be a great future reference and who will want to do business with the project team again.

4. Starting an Organizing Business

Now that you understand the professional organizing business and you have reviewed the concepts of personal, residential, and business organization, you should have a clearer idea of where you and your business will fit in.

In this chapter you will learn how to plan for and start up your own organizing business, from concept to bookkeeping to licensing to hiring staff. This information will set the stage for Chapter 5, where you'll learn how to market and sell your services to clients.

4.1 Preparing Yourself

Before you start your organizing business, it's valuable to learn about the business and prepare yourself to be a part of it. Professional organizers will tell you that they are always on the lookout for new information. Staying aware of what's new and trendy will help you to maintain your skills and knowledge base, and have insight to pass along to clients who will see you as an expert.

4.1.1 Print Resources

There is a wealth of information in print about organizing. Professionals in the organizing industry are always coming up with new ways to organize and new books are constantly being released on the subject.

Organizing is also a hot topic in newspapers and popular magazines. Your sources of print information will likely include the bookstore, for information you want to keep as a resource, and the library, for general information you can retain on your own or refer to clients.

The Bookstore

Just like there are different organizing specialties you can pursue as a professional organizer, there are also many books on how to organize in each specialty area. Before you focus on a specific area of organization, it's a good idea to survey what's out there with a few "bookstore days."

Give yourself some browsing time to open books, read introductions, and skim tables of contents. Read the backs of books, too, and any information you can find about authors, who are likely running organizing businesses. Try to find authors who have businesses you would like to emulate. When you have had a chance to browse, don't overwhelm yourself by buying a whole bunch of books at once. It's not cost-effective and it's stressful. Start with a few books that you feel approach organization in a way that's a fit for you.

You can also make a booklist of titles you'd like to add to your collection, and pick up a few every month. Include some details or a brief review of the book on the list to jog your memory in case it is a while before you purchase it. Make sure you include:

- The title

- The author

- The price to purchase

- A paragraph or two about the main topic

- Notes on its strong and weak points

The Library

Don't waste your time at a little library that won't have anything you need. The library with the biggest and best selection is the best place to go to save time. Some library systems also have catalogs you can peruse online, and place holds on material you pick up as it becomes available.

> **TIP:** Keep in mind that library books are not always the most current resources, but are usually books that have proven themselves over time. For new titles or hot new trends, you'll likely have to buy new.

Unlike a bookstore, you can bring back library books you don't like, so take out as many as you want. You can review them briefly, and return any that are not helpful. This is a great technique for building a list of resources you can recommend to clients for further study, especially the ones who don't want to spend a bunch of money on new books. Libraries are also great places to browse for and photocopy articles from magazines and newspapers, so you can add them to an idea file for later.

You can start a library booklist a lot like your bookstore list. Think about why you would recommend a book to a client. How would the book help a client with a particular organizing issue? Once again, write a brief review of a book to jog your memory later.

4.1.2 The Internet

The Internet has become a "cyber watering hole" for those in the profession, and a great place to see what other people are doing with their organizing businesses to inspire your own creative ideas.

Where to Start?

A great place to start your Internet search is the National Association of Professional Organizers (NAPO) website. This site gives you access to the websites of hundreds of NAPO members — professional organizers in every specialty from around the nation. You can find the membership list at **www.association-office.com/napo/referral/index.cfm**.

You can also try the Professional Organizers Web Ring Member Directory, which has some additional listings at **www.organizerswebring.com/ members/default.asp**.

You can bookmark your favorite websites so you can return to those you really like and read the content thoroughly. Create a folder called "PO websites" and then use subfolders to help you remember what you like about it, such as:

- Organizing ideas

- Marketing ideas

- Client ideas

- Training ideas

- Product ideas

- Website ideas

Learn to Read Critically

You can evaluate the sites to get a sense of whether or not your own ideas are right for the industry based on what you see, and you can see how they market their ideas and products. You can also buy products to use with your own clients that some professional organizers sell.

As you check out other organizers' websites, use the following questions to help you determine what aspects you might want to emulate or avoid:

- What is great about this website?

- What do you think makes it attractive to clients?

- How information-intensive is it?

- Can you learn something from it about organizing?

- What do you think of the language used on the site?

- Can you learn something from it about setting up your own business?

- Are the marketing techniques used on the site ones that you would consider?

- How successfully does the website "sell" you on services and products?

- Would you buy products or services from this organizer? Why or why not?

What you can't do is plagiarize sites and take their information and use it as your own. Take a survey of ideas that are out there, and use them to assist you in developing your own particular spin on organizing that makes your business unique and special.

4.1.3 Mentoring

One of the best ways to prepare yourself to open your own professional organizing business is to learn from people in the know. Doing so will also set you up for future networking, a business technique we'll explain later in the guide.

Most people are surprisingly willing to share information about what they do with those who ask. Many will do it free of charge, though some will charge a consultation fee for their services.

A mentoring relationship will allow you to connect with a working professional organizer who can offer you advice and guidance. Some will offer one-time mentoring in the form of an informational interview, while others will agree to become long-term advisors and professional contacts. It is all a matter of allowing a professional connection to progress naturally.

You can find professional organizers to learn from across North America by using the Internet. Just search on the phrase "professional organizer" or use the NAPO website or the Professional Organizers Web Ring mentioned earlier.

You can investigate potential mentoring relationships with a polite initial inquiry as to whether or not an organizer would be open to answering a few questions for you. Some will have time to talk with you and are glad to do it, and others are just too busy or will prefer not to for whatever reason. This is to be expected. Don't give up if you get a few negative responses to start with; there will be someone you connect with.

Sample Mentoring Request

Dear Ollie Organizer,

Hello, my name is Brianna Beginner. I am considering opening my own professional organizing business in Mytown, USA, and I am in the process of gathering information about how to go about doing it. I have spent a lot of time researching the industry and have had a chance to look at many websites. I was extremely impressed with yours.

Would you be willing to chat with me on the phone and answer a couple of questions I have about starting my own professional organizing business? I am planning on working in the Mytown area because my background in teaching at the local school gives me a lot of experience and knowledge to draw from, as well as contacts for future business.

If you are willing to answer a few questions for me I would be happy to call you at my expense and, of course, at your convenience. Or, if you prefer, we could have this discussion by email. I am happy to do whatever works best for you.

Ollie, I really appreciate you taking the time to read this letter. I look forward to hearing from you.

Sincerely,
Brianna Beginner

When you find someone who is willing to advise you on starting an organizing business, remember to:

- Be brief and limit your questions

- Be respectful of their time

- Know exactly what you want to ask

- Express gratitude for their help

It is important to plan the time you get to spend with unpaid mentors. Don't just call them or email them with vague remarks or questions, know what you want to ask going in. Spend some time and determine just a couple of important questions you would like to ask. By being prepared you won't waste the time of a busy professional organizer who is willing to help you out.

4.1.4 Personal Training and Coaching

Some professional organizers openly offer products, consulting services, training and apprentice programs to help others get started in this business — for a fee, of course. You may find that it is simpler and faster for you to approach someone who sells this service rather than search for professional organizers who will mentor you for free. There are three organizers listed below who offer training services to new organizers.

Remember, when you are paying for a product or a service, you should get a clear understanding of what you are buying, how much it will cost, how long it will take, and what results you can expect. Compare the various training and paid mentoring opportunities you see. People who have prepared something they are proud of will be willing to tell you about it, clear about the cost, and willing to share success stories from clients who have used it.

Professional Coaching: Barry Izsak

Barry Izsak describes his coaching services:

"I offer coaching services to those who are new to the industry and for those who want to take their business to the next level. The coaching services I provide are customized to the individual and their respective needs. I assist professional organizers in getting their business up and running quickly and save them countless hours of frustration 'spinning their wheels' on things that don't work — ultimately saving them lots of

time and money. In most cases, the time and money saved will more than cover the cost of our coaching services. I schedule a complimentary consultation to assess how I can best assist them and how to proceed."

You can read about Barry's services at **www.arrangingitall.com/content/ services/about_coaching.html**.

Telephone Coaching: Karen Ussery

"I coach new organizers in getting their businesses up and running. When I work with them before they have clients, it cuts their learning curve time so much."

— Karen Ussery, Organized For Success

A business organizer and trainer, Karen Ussery has a coaching business for new organizers. As a veteran organizer, she helps new organizers through the beginning planning phases of their businesses. She coaches them by telephone in three phone sessions a month, and also offers support by email as needed.

Her goal is to take an organizer from someone just beginning their business to someone who is actively and successfully seeing clients in three months, although students do have the option of extending the coaching period as well. Karen asks for a three-month commitment from her student organizers.

For more information visit **www.organizedforsuccess.com** and click on "Become a Professional Organizer" in the Resources section of the page.

Training Modules: Ramona Creel

"We have developed a training program… that is 12 modules, helping an organizer get started right from the very beginning. The program is in PDF format and can be printed off for new organizers to use at their leisure."

— Ramona Creel, OnlineOrganizing.com

Professional organizer Ramona Creel, owner of OnlineOrganizing.com and recipient of the NAPO Organizer's Choice Award for Best Organizing Service for 2003-2005, offers a series of training modules that give instruction and advice.

You can access an outline of each module online explaining what each one covers. The modules are available individually or in groups, allowing beginning professional organizers to purchase what they feel is the most relevant for them. The program also offers a certificate of completion.

For a full description of the program visit The Online Organizing Academy at **www.onlineorganizing.com/BecomeAnOrganizer.asp**.

4.1.5 Join a Professional Association

A professional organizer in the United States can get connected with industry experts through the National Association of Professional Organizers (NAPO); the Canadian organizer can do the same with Professional Organizers in Canada (POC).

Both associations also have regional or local chapter groups. As of the publication of this guide, NAPO has 25 chapters nationwide, and POC has 12. Both groups are seeing rapid growth as organizing continues to be a flourishing industry.

National Association of Professional Organizers (NAPO)

Website: **www.napo.net**
Phone: (847) 375-4746

Since 1985 this organization has spearheaded the coming together of those in this industry. NAPO is the largest association for professional organizers in the world, with more than 3,000 members from the United States and all parts of the globe. They offer a variety of benefits and the credibility of a professional affiliation with the organizing industry.

"We want to help people that are entering the business to be the best professional organizers that they can be. Our goal is to elevate the professionalism within the industry," says Barry Izsak, current president of NAPO.

Membership Cost

It costs $200 dollars annually for a regular membership. An associate membership is also available to those who sell, distribute, or manufacture goods or services that organizers use.

Benefits

Benefits include:

- Information about association member companies from which you can purchase organizing equipment and supplies

- Networking opportunities

- Added credibility for your business

- Discounted fees for the annual trade show and conference event

- Ongoing educational opportunities

- Online referral service

- A national membership directory

- Support from national NAPO staff members to the local chapter organizations

- Subscription to the NAPO News

Education

One of the goals of NAPO is to create a comprehensive curriculum and certification program for the organizing industry. Their core competencies are the areas of knowledge that they have determined a professional organizer should have to be successful. NAPO offers a variety of courses including classroom and telecourses, including a telecourse for those new to professional organizing.

For more information visit **www.napo.net**. The address for the NAPO Core Competencies page is **www.napo.net/get_organized/education/core_comp.html**.

A Local NAPO Meeting

The Arizona Chapter of NAPO was gracious enough to allow FabJob author Grace Jasmine the chance to survey one of their meetings, held at a local restaurant. Here is a description of the experience.

When I arrived I was welcomed by their friendly greeters and asked to join them in a large area of the restaurant that they reserve for their monthly meetings. After the initial business, Dorothy Breininger, National Membership Director for NAPO, presented the group with their charter member certificate to formalize their induction into NAPO as the 19th national chapter.

Ms. Breininger gave the local chapter information about what was new and interesting at NAPO, including continued work to create a certification process for NAPO members nationwide. The representative also took a very hands-on approach with members and made it clear to them that she was personally available by phone to interact with them, help them with questions, or even give them that sometimes necessary pep talk.

Lunch was ordered and served as members were asked to review their member entries in the National Directory of Professional Organizers. Members then had an opportunity to stand and briefly introduce themselves and their businesses. I noticed that most professional organizers had interesting, brief presentations and catchy slogans to help you remember their specialty.

Next a guest speaker, Victoria Mikoch, a private investigator, spoke on issues of paper security management and identity theft — important for professional organizers who work with clients who are disposing of documentation. Members were asked to complete a survey regarding the presentation, and then invited to network and mingle. Meanwhile, Golden Circle Members (those who have been working professionally in the industry for more than five years) met and had a brief meeting of their own.

Overall, I found the group to be a motivated, successful and charming group of people — experts at their businesses, and more than willing to share insights and referrals with one another.

Tradeshows and Events

The 2006 NAPO Annual National Conference & Organizing Expo was held March 22-25 in Boston, Massachusetts. The 2007 conference is slated for April 25-28 in Minneapolis, Minnesota. The conferences include a variety of speakers, networking opportunities, seminars and events.

January is GO Month (or "Get Organized" Month), an annual event created by NAPO to heighten awareness about organization on a national level. Hundreds of events are sponsored during GO Month in January by local chapters throughout the nation.

Local Chapters

There are 25 local NAPO chapters available to join. A list of them and contact information is provided at the end of this guide. (Note that you may be required to join at the national level first.)

If, when you start your organizing business, you experience a sense of isolation, your local NAPO chapter offers instant access to other professionals in the organizing industry. Other benefits include access to the advice, referrals, information, and opinions of others in your industry, support, community awareness and how it will affect your business, and networking opportunities.

Professional Organizers in Canada (POC)

"We started as a couple of people in Toronto and we now have chapters across Canada. Professional organizing is a really fast-growing field in Canada and many of our members are also members of NAPO. Our mission is to spread the word about organizing and to support other organizers."

— Laurene Livesey Park, former president,
Professional Organizers of Canada

Website: **www.organizersincanada.com**
Email: inquiries@OrganizersInCanada.com

In Canada the national association is Professional Organizers in Canada, or POC. Since 1999, POC has been meeting as a group dedicated to providing a support network for professional organizers throughout

Canada. POC is a web-based organization, run by members for members to provide "increased visibility and professionalism" for their profession. Membership to date is over 300 strong, and rapidly expanding.

Membership Cost

New members can join online using the website's membership form and using a credit card for membership fees. The annual dues are $180 with a one-time processing fee of $50. Depending upon when you join in the year, the membership fee is prorated. POC's membership year begins on March 1, and membership fees are due annually at that time.

Benefits

POC membership benefits include:

- Access to members-only website

- Networking opportunities

- A member directory

- An online referral service

- Invitation to attend an annual conference

- Ongoing educational opportunities

- A newsletter

A unique benefit to members is access to promotional materials that members can purchase to show their affiliation to POC and to give to potential clients during the course of client consultations. The website has an ordering form for a variety of products that lend credibility to their business.

Education

By clicking on the Education/Seminars link on the POC website you can see a variety of POC-sponsored and approved classes that are available. There are live classes and seminars as well as teleconference classes and distance learning opportunities. An offering of interest is a one-hour teleconference designed for those who are considering becoming professional organizers, conducted by an experienced professional organizer.

Trade Shows and Events

POC has an annual conference featuring a variety of speakers and workshops, allowing members to stay current on new developments and education in professional organizing. The 2006 conference was held October 19-21 in Toronto, ON. POC also sponsors an annual national event called NOWeek! (National Organizing Week), traditionally held the first week of May.

Local POC Chapters

Like NAPO, Professional Organizers in Canada also has local chapters. As of this writing there are nine chapters throughout Canada. You will find contact information for POC local chapters at the end of this guide.

4.1.6 Small Business Resources

There are plenty of ways to acquire new business skills even while you are in the process of opening your business.

The Small Business Administration

The Small Business Administration is a government organization dedicated to giving support to American small business owners. One important part of the SBA's offerings is their Small Business Training Network E-Business Institute that allows small business owners to take online courses free of charge. Topics include Starting a Business, Business Management, Marketing and Advertising, Financing, and Employee Management. Visit **www.sba.gov/training** for more information.

They also have a library with more than 200 free business publications. This is a wonderful free resource for the small businessperson. The web address for the library is **www.sba.gov/training/library.html**.

To learn about other SBA programs and services, visit their website at **www.sbaonline.sba.gov** or call the SBA Small Business Answer Desk at 800-U-ASK-SBA (800-827-5722).

SCORE — Counselors to America's Small Business

SCORE is an organization of retired business executives that act as consultants for your business free of charge — all you need to do is contact your local SCORE office and make an appointment. To make the best use of your consulting appointment, it is important to try to match your needs with someone who has experience in a similar industry, and to go into a consulting appointment with clear and ready questions.

SCORE also offers a variety of classes and some supplementary materials that you can purchase for a small fee. Visit **www.score.org** or call 800-634-0245 to find the nearest SCORE location.

Online Small Business Workshop

The Canadian government offers an Online Small Business Workshop at **www.cbsc.org/osbw** which includes information about taxes, financing, incorporation, and other topics.

Industry Professionals and Consultants

Another option to learn the things you need to learn is to hire someone to help you, teach you, or otherwise prepare you to deal with the part of your business in which they are experts. These are people that you will pay for their services, but they can teach you a lot. You can hire any of the following people to assist you with your business:

- Computer consultants

- Web designers

- Accountants

- Attorneys

- Graphic design consultants

- Printing professionals

Learning on Your Own

All community colleges and junior colleges have business courses. Many have courses designed to help new business owners learn new skills. Most of them have basic classes in issues that concern small business owners like accounting, finance, marketing and sales, and more. Online, a list of colleges can be found at **www.mcli.dist.maricopa.edu/cc**.

4.2 Setting Up Your Business

Once you've learned about the industry in general, you are ready to start moving forward with the things you need to do to set up your business. In this section you will learn how to:

- Plan your concept

- Set your goals

- Write a business plan

- Evaluate your start-up costs

- Get financing, if needed

- Choose a business name and structure

- Evaluate your insurance needs and tax situation

- Set up your office to start working

4.2.1 Your Business Concept

You have the power to create the business you want to have, exactly the way you want it to be. This is one of the great things about being self-employed in such a creative and unusual business. It's an exciting prospect, but maybe a little overwhelming. In the following sections you will get a chance to do the thinking and imagining part of starting your own business as you formulate and then define your ideas.

Brainstorming Ideas

You already have one excellent idea — and that is to open your own professional organizing business. Now you will move forward from this main idea to a variety of related ideas that will help you define your business.

How do you come up with ideas for your new business? When you begin, you must be both imaginative and nonjudgmental. Let your mind run wild thinking of any and all possibilities. The ideas you think of don't necessarily have to make sense. They don't have to be orderly, or even things you will ultimately consider doing.

Brainstorming is the act of letting your ideas flow quickly and easily — it is spontaneous imagining. After you have a lot of ideas there will be plenty of time to pick and choose among them.

If you haven't had a chance in previous careers to do much brainstorming, sometimes it is helpful to start with broad categories. Begin the process using a blank sheet of paper labeled only with the words "My Business Ideas" and see where your imagination takes you. If you get stuck, you can try answering some specific questions like the ones below.

- What is my organizing specialty?

- What services will I provide?

- Who do I want to work with?

- Where will I work?

- How will I find clients?

- How will I present my services to potential clients?

- What will a typical work day be like?

- How will I network, and with whom?

- Will I have a logo? A slogan? A theme?

- What specific things about my business will be unique?

After you have written some descriptive answers to the questions above, read them over and enhance them where necessary. Try to make these descriptions as vivid and as complete as you can, as they are the building blocks of your business planning.

Don't worry if you don't feel like you can give complete answers to all of these questions just yet. Even answers you feel sure of now will change as you gather knowledge and gain experience. You can always change your plans based on what you have learned.

A Vision Statement

Your vision statement will be simple, but powerful. It is an affirmation about what your business will be in the future, stated in the present tense. Lots of successful people from athletes to scientists use vision statements in the process of affirmation, to add power to their dreams for their own success.

In the brainstorming exercise you had a chance to work on your mental picture of your business. You thought about what you want to do, and how you want to do it. A vision statement allows you to refine those thoughts into a simple and useable statement that helps you envision your business in the future.

Take a look at the statements you made in the brainstorming exercise, and synthesize them into a sentence or two in the present tense about your business, as you would like to see it in the future. Here is an example for a service aimed at new moms:

> "I have a lucrative, busy business called "The Organized Baby" helping new mothers and their families organize their homes, baby equipment, and schedules. I sell clients my insight, hands-on help, new products, and the published organizational materials I create."

A vision statement is something you can use as a motivating tool. You can change it as you change your ideas, and you can rewrite it anytime you want to. It should be read every day to help you envision your business as you would like it to be.

4.2.2 Setting Business Goals

Setting goals and smaller tasks you want to accomplish will help you get your business running and successful as quickly as possible. You can refer back to the forms found in Chapter 3 to help set your own business goals: the *Goal Statement Form*, the *Major Tasks Planner*, and the *Task Breakdown Worksheet*. Samples of each will appear in this section to guide you.

Your Goal Statement

Remember that a goal statement should be powerful, programmed, precise and practical. Consider if your goal was:

"To open my own professional organizing business serving residential clients."

Once you pin your goal down, add words that will make your goal powerful and motivating. Consider words that add excitement and description to your goal. If your sentence makes you see it and feel it, you are on the right track. For example:

My goal is to…

"Open my own highly successful, lucrative professional organizing business called Serenity Solutions in which I specialize in serving residential clients with all aspects of their home organization needs, write articles and books, and become a locally known public speaker by eight months from today's date."

Write your goal on nice paper, cut it out and place the goal affirmation card somewhere you will see it every day.

Setting Tasks

The steps for how to set tasks have been reprinted here from Chapter 2 so you can easily refer to them again.

- Set the goal (as detailed above)

- Write down the major tasks on the *Major Tasks Planner*

- Put the tasks in chronological order

- Fill out the *Task Breakdown Worksheet* to determine minor tasks

- Estimate the time that each minor task will take to complete, and add the time for all the minor tasks to arrive at a tentative completion time for a major task

- Add the total times for the completion for each major task and you will have an estimated time for the ultimate goal

- Create a master schedule and calendar to determine what to do when

---

Sample Major Tasks Planner

Ultimate Goal:
Open a highly successful, lucrative professional organizing business called Serenity Solutions in which I specialize in serving residential clients with all aspects of their home organization needs, write articles and books, and become a locally known public speaker by eight months from today's date.

Tasks:
Major tasks needed to complete goal:

1. Set up the legal aspects of my business including getting a business license, and making sure no one else has my business name. Look into incorporating.

---

2. Get a small business loan (if needed) for computer equipment in my home office, and purchase new computer equipment.

3. Join my local chapter of NAPO. Start attending meetings so I can network with some other organizers and learn about the business from them. Also, take some educational courses through NAPO.

4. Get business cards, stationery, and a brochure. To make my own brochure, take a night class on desktop publishing for business that I saw at the local community college.

5. Join Toastmasters to perfect my speaking skills. Plan and practice some presentations on organization that I can later use for speaking engagements. Start to speak professionally in 4 months.

6. Set up my new office in the extra bedroom. Set up my bookkeeping software and my contact database.

7. Practice organizing the homes of some of my friends and family to perfect my skills. Maybe do the first few for free, and then do the next few friends at a large discount.

8. Create documents that outline my services and my prices and include a guarantee and work agreements.

9. Get some press for my business. Write a press release about opening my new business, and establish contact with local press.

10. Find five networking organizations and become active in all of them. Work at marketing my business by networking at these organizations.

Sample Task Breakdown Worksheet

Major Task Description #1:
Set up the legal aspects of my business.

Smaller Tasks:	Estimated Completion Time
1. Get a business license	1–4 weeks
2. Check about my business name	1 month
3. Create the legal structure for my business	3 months
Total estimated time:	1–3 months
Total estimated cost:	TBD

Notes:
I need to get an attorney. I have to find about publishing my fictitious business name. I should secure my domain name for my website.

Major Task Description #2:
Get a small business loan for computer equipment.

Smaller Tasks:	Estimated Completion Time
1. Research equipment cost	2 months
2. Write business plan	2 months
3. Meet with lender	3 months
4. Purchase new equipment	After loan approval
Total estimated time:	TBD
Total estimated cost:	TBD

Notes:
Have to do research for business plan and then get loan.
Consider going to credit union for small loan, $2,000 max.
Make back up plan in case I can't get a loan or decide not to.

Major Task Description #3:
Join NAPO local chapter.

Smaller Tasks:	Estimated Completion Time
1. Go on website and join using a credit card.	1 hour
2. Check out local chapter and attend a meeting.	1 day
3. Join chapter.	1 day

Total estimated time:	TBD
Total estimated cost:	TBD

Notes:
Want to get to know a certain number of members at each meeting for networking purposes.

After determining the smaller tasks and their estimated times, go back to the major task worksheets and fill in total estimated times for major tasks and milestones. Add these together to determine estimated times it will take to complete your ultimate goals.

Master Calendar

After you have filled out the *Goal Statement Form*, the *Major Tasks Planner*, and the *Task Breakdown Worksheet*, you are ready to schedule your major tasks. To do this you will need your calendar.

Begin by starting with your proposed end date or the day you want to be actually running your business. (In the sample, that was eight months from the current date.) Now, work backwards. Decide what has to be done first, second, third and so on, and also what tasks can be done simultaneously.

It is natural when you have a number of milestones to complete in any goal process that some tasks will overlap. You can use a Gantt chart like the one on the next page to organize your overlapping milestone tasks.

One-Year Gantt Chart

Month

Tasks

4.2.3 Creating a Business Plan

One of the most common reasons for making a business plan is to attempt to secure financing, but even if you won't need a loan to start your business, creating a business plan is a helpful planning exercise. A business plan that isn't designed to obtain financing is sometimes called an annual plan.

A business plan is an organized, well-researched look at each aspect of your business. A good business plan gets you to take a look at things that you might forget otherwise. Your business plan will include:

- A table of contents

- An executive summary

- A business description

- A market analysis

- A marketing plan

- A financial plan and statements

- Appendices

Table of Contents

A table of contents will let readers move through your business plan with ease. The best way to make the table of contents is to write the rest of your business plan, and then write or review your table of contents last.

Executive Summary

An executive summary is a one or two page summary of the rest of your plan to come. You may find it is easiest to write this portion of your business plan at the end of the process — in essence, to "sum up" your plan.

Business Description

The business description outlines all aspects of your business clearly. The simplified way of looking at this part of the business plan is to describe what you are planning to do and how you are planning to do it. Describe your business — the area you will operate in, what services you will offer, and their features. Discuss products you are going to sell and where you will get them. If you have a team, who are they, and why will they be an asset in making your business a fantastic success?

Market Analysis

A market analysis is a look at the market for professional organizing businesses, how you will position yours in the marketplace, and who your competition and customers will be. You will use statistics and data to explain why there is a need for your business.

Marketing Plan

In your marketing plan you explain what will make your business unique. If you use a business plan for a loan, lenders will want to see that you have thought about your business' potential place in the marketplace carefully and that you have devised a plan to be successful.

Financial Plan and Statements

How much money do you need to open and sustain your business until you show a profit? Here you see how much you think it will cost to operate your organizing business, what you expect your sales to be, and what profit margin you expect. This portion of the plan is the place for real numbers. You will need statements to back up your projections, such as a projected income statement, a projected balance sheet, and a projected cash-flow analysis.

Appendices

The appendices include all of the documents that support your claims. Include your personal credit history, any completed loan applications if you are using the business plan to secure financing, your team's resumes, and any materials that help you present your business. You might have a copy of your brochure and your business license.

The following resources can help you with more information and samples to guide you through this planning process. You might also consider hiring a business consultant if you plan to apply for financing with your plan.

- *Bplan.com — Business Plan Software and Sample Business Plans*
  www.bplans.com

- *SBA: Starting Business — Writing the Plan*
  www.sba.gov/starting_business/planning/writingplan.html

4.2.4 Financing Your Business

Compared to many other businesses, opening your organizing business will require only a small initial investment of money, likely to be supplied by your personal savings. Depending on how you grow, or your ultimate goals, you may want to get a loan at some point to grow your business the way you want. This might involve approaching a lending institution or investors, so you'll want to be prepared.

How Much Will You Need?

Remember to include the following items in your budgets. The start-up budget includes all the costs necessary to get your business up and running. Operating costs are ongoing expenses, such as advertising, utilities, and rent. Some expenses appear on both lists.

Start-up budget

- Legal and professional fees

- Licenses and permits

- Office equipment

- Insurance

- Office supplies

- Advertising and promotions

- Accounting expenses

- Any training you want to pursue

Operating budget (First 3 to 6 months)

- Your salary

- Insurance

- Rent/portion of mortgage

- Loan repayments

- Advertising and promotions

- Legal and accounting fees

- Ongoing supplies

- Utility payments

- Dues and subscriptions

- Taxes

Experts suggest that it takes at least a year for a new business to begin to make a profit, which means that if you're just starting out, you should plan to live on your savings or other income (not from the business) for at least six months while your business is getting off the ground.

Sources of Funding

You can use any mixture you want of the financing suggestions below, such as your own savings, a family loan, and/or a small business loan. The most important thing is to make sure you agree to loan repayment terms that are realistic for you.

Your Own Savings

Never forget that you might be your own best source of funding. To raise your own capital you can cash out stocks, bonds, life insurance, an IRA, or retirement account, increase your credit on charge cards, use savings, take out a second mortgage on your house, or sell something that is valuable like a car, jewelry, real estate, or art.

Family and Friends

One of the greatest resources for your start-up money will always be the people you know who believe in you and your ideas — your family and friends. Very often they will help you with money when all other resources fail you, they usually will agree to payback terms that aren't as strict as commercial lenders... and they are usually pulling for you, too.

As with any other kind of loan, it is important to make sure that you and your family member or friend completely understand and agree to the terms of the loan. Make sure it is a written document so you both have an understanding of exactly when and how you will pay the loan back.

Another possibility is to ask a family member to co-sign a commercial loan for you. Co-signing means that this person agrees to take on the financial responsibility of the loan if you should fail, and family members are often willing to help you out this way.

Investors

For some new business owners, finding a person who wants to partner with them, share the responsibility of their new business, and who will bring some money to invest, too, is the perfect solution. Investors are looking to make money by investing in your business. You have to assure them that they will get something out of it, because for them investing in your business isn't personal (like it might be when a family member invests in your business), it is business.

Investors work one of two ways: they want to see their initial money returned with a profit, or they want to own part of your business. You have to decide if you feel you will be able to meet the terms of the investor and if you want to share ownership of your business with another person.

A Bank Loan

Commercial loans are loans that you can get from a financial institution like a bank or a credit union. The terms of your loan will depend upon several things, including your credit score, your collateral, and your ability to pay back a loan.

If you need only a small amount of money – a couple of thousand, maybe – you may be able to secure a small personal loan or line of credit from your regular bank or credit union.

As you learned in the previous section, a business plan will help lenders decide whether or not to give you a loan, but for a relatively small loan, they are much more interested in your personal financial status. They will look at how much money you need every month to pay your bills, what kind of resources or assets you have, what kind of debt you are in, and how you will repay this debt while you are putting your total effort into opening your business.

Other Options

It might not be the best time for you to start a business, for either financial or personal reasons. If so, you might consider partnering or starting part-time until you are ready to take off and fly.

If you are interested in getting your feet wet as a professional organizer but you aren't quite ready to make an investment of your time and money to start your own business, consider these ideas:

- *Network.* Meet people at NAPO chapter meetings and let it be known that you are hoping to join another existing business as an employee. The more you talk with other people, the more likely you will find the right opportunity for you. Another way to get the word out is to send out an exploratory email to organizer businesses in your area or call. Some professional organizers hire staff, especially occasional or part-time people to help them. It never hurts to ask.

- *Partner.* Consider joining an existing business as a partner. Ask around and see if anyone is interested in taking on a business partner, or ask your friends or family members to start an organizing business with you, cutting the risk and time investment in half.

Ways to Get Help

The SBA

The Small Business Administration (SBA) doesn't actually lend you money, but they may guarantee a loan that a commercial lender will give you. In essence, the SBA gives lenders the reassurance that they will pay back the loan if you don't. The SBA must be convinced that your loan is a good risk, and you must apply for an SBA loan in order to access these commercial lenders that partner with the SBA. For information visit **www.sba.gov/financing**. You can read an overview of "SBA Financing Basics" at **www.sba.gov/financing/basics/basics.html**.

SBA Online Women's Business Center

The SBA has a division aimed at women called the SBA's Office of Women's Business Ownership. This special division of the SBA promotes the growth of women-owned businesses. Their website at **www.onlinewbc.gov** has excellent business information in seven languages that can be accessed and used by anyone who needs information about starting their business.

In particular, the finance section at **www.sba.gov/financing/index.html** gives step-by-step clear instructions on almost every financial aspect of opening a new business. While this site is geared toward women, the advice and practical information is some of the best available anywhere and valuable for every new business owner.

4.2.5 Choosing a Business Name

Choosing a business name is one of the most important steps in getting ready to open your own business. Unfortunately it isn't quite as easy as dreaming up a new name and saying, "That's it!" Here are some things to consider when choosing your name.

Does It Tell People What You Do?

If you open an organizing business that specializes in relocation jobs and you call yourself "Organizing for Everyone," your customers will not be aware of your specialty. Naming your business "Purge Then Pack — Moving Consultants" will get your point across. Your business name will speak for your business when you aren't available to do so. Consider choosing a name that lets people know immediately what you do.

Is It Catchy?

Will people remember it? Is it attention-grabbing, or unusual, or fun?

Does it relate to your business niche or specialty? Pick a name that arouses interest, is clever, or will appeal to your clients. Curiosity can catch paying clients!

Is It Based on Something You Might Decide to Change?

If you name your business "Only Offices," there might come a time that you begin to service self-employed people in their homes, and your name will no longer reflect what you are trying to sell. If your business morphs over time, will your name still be relevant?

Is the Name Used by Anyone Else?

You have to make sure that there is no other business operating with the same name, or even a name that is similar to the extent that a business owner might feel your business name is detracting from them.

The first place to look is your local phone book, then check with your county clerk's office. If you are going to incorporate your business, you will need to check your name with your Secretary of State's office to be sure that your name hasn't already been taken.

Do You Love It?

Ultimately you are the person who will need to live with your business name. It should be one that you feel great about. It should feel like it fits and it should make you happy.

Filing Your Name

Unless the name you choose for your business is your own name, you will have to file what is known as a DBA ("Doing Business As") or a fictitious business statement.

How you file a fictitious business name varies from place to place, so it is best to call your local city or county clerk's office to check the requirements in your area. They will give you all the details, information about the associated costs, and let you know if you will need to have your fictitious business name published in your local newspaper.

TIP: If you decide to form a corporation, the legal documents that you file as part of that process will serve the same purpose as filing a fictitious business statement.

A helpful resource is offered at **www.nolo.com**. (Click on "Business & Human Resources," then "Starting a Business," then "Naming Your Business.")

4.2.6 Legal Matters

Before you start your business, you will need to make sure that all the necessary legal documents are completed. Here's what you'll need.

Licensing

No matter what kind of company you own, you may need a business license. There may also be other permits and licenses you will need, so contact your local city hall or county clerk's office. Contact information can be found in your phone book or online at sites such as **www.sba.gov/hotlist/license.html** or **www.entrepreneur.com** (use the search feature at entrepreneur.com to search for "Business Licenses and Permits.")

Legal Structure

There are up to four ways to set up the legal structure for a business in the U.S. or Canada. They include:

- Sole proprietorship
- Partnership
- Corporation
- Limited liability company

Sole Proprietorship

As a sole proprietor you will be the sole owner of your business. It is usually the easiest way for a new business owner to get started, and a common choice for professional organizers. As a sole proprietor, you are personally responsible for all business liability, so make sure you are adequately insured. Sole proprietors may hire employees, but are liable for anything an employee does while working for them, and are responsible for filing the appropriate tax forms.

To be a sole proprietor all you need to do is make sure that you have obtained the necessary licenses for running your business on a city, county, state/provincial and federal level.

Partnership

Just as the name implies, a partnership means that you share legal and financial responsibilities of your business with one or more partners. This can be a good thing, but there are also some associated risks.

TIP: If you want to run the business yourself, but need a partner to contribute money, a limited partnership might be the right option for you. In this arrangement the "general partner" is the person who runs the business, and a "limited partner" provides capital.

You will need to have a partnership agreement that spells out every aspect of what you both agree to do to open and run your new business. It is a good idea to hire an attorney to help you complete a partnership agreement and advise you about any potential areas of conflict.

You should:

• Decide who owns what. You need to decide who owns what percentage of the business. Sometimes you will not want a 50-50 split, but some other division of ownership.

• Decide who does what. As partners you will need to discuss ahead of time who will be responsible for each aspect of the business.

• Decide who contributes what. What portion of the start-up and running costs will each partner be responsible for? The percentage of start-up cash invested is one way to determine the percentage of ownership of the business.

- Decide who earns what. How much money will you and your partner take from the business for salary? How will this change over time based on profits?

- Decide who decides. What do you do if you can't agree? Are there some decisions that will be handled by one partner? How will you handle a disagreement about an important decision?

Corporation

A corporation is an entity that is not directly connected to your personal finances or wealth. In the case of lawsuit, the corporation is sued and not the individuals. Many people choose a corporation for this reason. In essence, you limit your personal liability.

If you form a corporation your business will have stock, which you can sell to stockholders to raise capital. If you sell stock you are accountable to your stockholders, but if you hold all your own stock than you can be personally liable for your company just as if you aren't incorporated. The bottom line is, get professional legal advice to make these kinds of decisions.

Limited Liability Company

A limited liability company is a relatively new type of business legal structure in the United States. It is a combination of a partnership and corporation, and it is considered to have some of the best attributes of both, including limited personal liability. Talk with a lawyer to find out if a LLC is right for you.

Taxes

Depending on the type of business structure you choose, you will either file as part of your personal taxes, or separately as your business. Many professional organizers have a professional handle their taxes to ensure things are handled properly and to their best advantage, but the more you know, the better position you are in to hire a good tax professional and provide them with the information they need.

The Internal Revenue Service (IRS) and the Canada Revenue Agency have a number of informative documents online (such as the ones listed below) that you can look at to learn the basics about everything you need for federal small business taxes.

- *IRS — Small Business and Self-Employed One-Stop Resource*
  www.irs.gov/businesses/small/index.html

- *IRS — Tax Guide for Small Businesses*
  www.irs.gov/pub/irs-pdf/p334.pdf

- *Canada Revenue Agency*
  Small Business and Self-Employed Individuals
  www.cra-arc.gc.ca/tax/business/menu-e.html

It is also important to be informed about your tax obligation on a state and local level. Tax laws and requirements vary on a state-by-state basis and locally, too. Bankrate.com has state-by-state links to more information at **www.bankrate.com/brm/itax/state/state_tax_home.asp**.

Insurance

Making sure you are properly insured is important, and in the case of Workers' Compensation insurance, it is the law. You must protect your business if you damage something in a client's home or office, you should insure your office equipment, and if you hire them, you must insure your employees.

Getting a Business Owner's Policy (a BOP) is often a good place to start. These policies are designed for small business owners with fewer than 100 employees and revenues of under $1 million, and combine liability and property insurance together. Small business owners like these policies because of their convenience and affordable premiums. You can read more about this topic at the Insurance Information Institute website at **www.iii.org/individuals/business**.

Workers' compensation insurance provides coverage in case an employee is injured or falls sick on the job. Workers' compensation insurance protects your workers and ultimately your business. This sort of coverage is legally required in all states except Texas. Workers' compensation insurance is also mandatory in Canada, but the rules and regulations vary depending upon the part of Canada in which your business is located.

- *Insure.com — Workers Compensation Insurance Law Tool*
  http://info.insure.com/business/workerscomp/lawtool.cfm

- *Small Business Canada—Workers Compensation Insurance*
  http://sbinfocanada.about.com/cs/workerscomp

You may also consider medical insurance designed for the self-employed and offer this, if you decide to, to your employees. Based on your business success, you may decide to pay a partial contribution along with the contribution of employees to make it possible for them to have insurance benefits as part of their employment package.

4.2.7 Your Office

Setting up your office space should be a fun and unique challenge — you will be "organizing" yourself. Because of the nature of the work, most professional organizers work out of their homes, and it's likely you will, too.

Having a home office can be a wonderful thing. There are so many benefits. You don't have to drive to work, you don't have to get dressed if you don't want to, getting lunch or a snack is a simple and economical matter, and getting home after work involves getting up and walking into another room.

With so much time spent onsite at the client's space, you'll have minimal needs for office space and time spent there, and the added cost of renting office space is unnecessary in most cases. However, if for some reason you are renting an office space, the majority of the advice in this section will still apply.

You will want to select and design a space that will really work for you, select furniture and equipment and supplies you will need to get started, and learn how to work effectively during your office hours, which can be a challenge for the self-employed. Let's go over the process.

Selecting a Space

"I turned a bedroom into an office. I have a highly technical husband who helps me with my computers and my website. I have a bookcase and filing cabinet and my closet has been converted into all shelving where I keep all my office and paper supplies... I am very organized; I don't have any clutter in here!"

— Brenda Clements, Professional Organizer

The first thing you will need to do is select the perfect space. Maybe you have a spare room just waiting for you to transform into an office. If not, consider the space that you do have and how it might work for an office. If you are short on space you can use part of a room that is used for another purpose.

Consider what you will do in your office space, and if it meets those needs. You might need the space in order to:

- Talk on the telephone

- Prepare marketing materials

- Work on your website

- Write articles or books

- Write speeches and presentations

- Prepare client materials

- Do the planning stages or the "think time" phase of a client job

- Prepare proposals, statements of work, and contracts

- Keep up with correspondence

- Do billing and bookkeeping

- Organize your schedule

- Prepare mailings of materials or products

- Occasionally meet with clients

When you work at home you will have many, many unavoidable distractions — it just comes with the territory. So remember to plan for this as you select a space. A space that is somewhat removed from the hustle and bustle of your family's daily life is the best choice. And, if at all possible, a space that you can separate from the rest of the house by a door will help you with interruptions and noise control.

You will be the person who ultimately spends a lot of time in this space; does it have the sort of features you need to make it a happy and productive space for you? For example, some people must have a window so they can see outside and don't feel claustrophobic; other people get distracted if they can look at anything other than their task at hand.

TIP: Before you decide on a place to locate your office, pull a chair into the proposed space and sit and try to picture how it would work as your home office space. This type of hands-on approach will help you identify potential pitfalls in advance.

Outfitting the Office

Furniture and Equipment

If you work from home, you can adapt many things you already have to work in your office space, which will not only be cost-effective, but also will make it easier to mesh with your existing furniture and ambiance.

Remember, you don't have to have traditional office furniture in your home office; you can have anything you want. You might have an old chest of drawers you adapt for supplies or files, or a closet that is adjacent to the space where you have built-in storage. The best thing to do is to use what you do have imaginatively.

Take a tour around your house and see what furniture and equipment you can adapt for your space. Then you will be ready to make a list to see what you will need to purchase. You may need some or all of the following for your office:

- A desk

- A comfortable chair

- Additional seating for clients

- Extra work space

- Lamps or other work-friendly lighting

- Storage for books and files

- A telephone (consider a speaker phone and/or a headset)

- A separate phone line

- An answering machine or service

- A computer

- A printer

- A shredder

Your software needs may include: word processing, scheduling, accounting, client database, presentation software, desktop publishing software, and web page software. You will also need to arrange for Internet access.

Office Supplies

Office supplies you may need include:

- Paper

- Presentation folders

- Printer cartridges

- Pens or pencils

- A three-hole punch

- Scissors

- Stapler and staples

- Note pads

- Files and folders

- Stationery

- Envelopes

- Postage supplies

- Business cards

- Post-its

- Recordable CDs or floppy disks

- Binders

- Binder dividers

- Storage containers

The Desk Apprentice, created by candidates on the television show *The Apprentice*, has a 360° swivel base and custom-made storage areas for a variety of office supplies including hanging file folders, staplers and notepads. Photo courtesy of Staples.

Form and Function

"I have everything where it is convenient — everything is at my fingertips."

— Chris McKenry, Professional Organizer

To make your home office really effective you have to have everything you need to do your work placed conveniently around you. While you may be able to store some supplies away from your space – especially if your space is small – you will definitely need everything you use on a regular basis at your fingertips.

Just like arranging any other room in your house you must pay attention to function (effective use of the space) and form (how it looks and if that makes you happy). You have to use it; you need to really like it. Don't overlook the following as you design your space:

- Ergonomic features

- Comfortable lighting

- Artwork you enjoy

- Plants

- A small tabletop fountain

- Instrumental background music

- Anything else that makes the space "happy" for you

The Home Worker's Challenges

There is one thing about the home office that hasn't been mentioned yet — the people who live in your house are not going to magically go away when you need to work.

Even if you live alone or your family will be gone during the day, there are more distractions that you might imagine: think about family, the phone, noisy neighbors, unexpected guests, door-to-door sales people, repair people, delivery service people, gardeners or landscapers, or even a malfunctioning smoke alarm!

You find ways to make it work, though. The author of this guide, now a home worker for 15 years, recalls her first home office experience:

"When I established my first home office my daughter was a babe-in-arms. She needed constant attention and I needed to work, too. I solved the dilemma by creating a baby station in my home office space. Basically, she moved in with me into the office space and we co-existed very nicely. At times she even slept in a baby carrier on my oversized desk.

As she grew she had a playpen and a television with toddler videos to watch during those times when I needed to work and she wasn't napping. Eventually I found ways for her to get involved, first with pretend tasks that were fun for her, and then with simple office-related tasks that were still fun for her but actually helped me. She loved being involved and feeling included — and I got work done at times when it might have been otherwise impossible."

The following tips may help others adjust to you as a home worker:

- Work after your children or spouse go to sleep, or while your family is at work or school

- Let friends know that although you are home, you are working and not available for visits or phone calls — get call display if you can

- Ask people not to drop by unannounced during your work day

These tips will help you adjust to being a home worker:

- Leave your office and work somewhere else when you can

- Don't run personal errands, do other household tasks or watch TV during work hours… you'll get sidetracked before you know it

- Take breaks or change tasks frequently

- Set office hours, and turn off the phone ringer or computer when you are not working — you work from home, but not 24 hours a day!

4.3 Operating Your Business

Running your business is more than helping clients get organized in their spaces. You must make sure that the business as a whole runs smoothly. This isn't as daunting as it seems at first. It is simply a matter of setting up the systems and procedures you want in place to accomplish your daily business objectives.

This section takes a look at getting a good operations system in place.

4.3.1 Scheduling Your Time

"I don't start working with clients until 9 or 10—I do phone calls [first]. I book one client a day, and 4 to 6 hours is usually the time I spend with a client…[although] a move-in day is a ten-hour day."

— Brenda Clements, Professional Organizer

Professional organizers have the freedom to determine their own daily schedules. Tasks you will likely be scheduling in include:

Promoting Your Business

- Scouting for new networking opportunities

- Attending networking functions

- Booking speaking dates

- Writing and planning presentations

- Working on your website

- Writing press releases or articles

- Writing or distributing tip books

Working With Clients

- Entering clients into your database

- Calling potential clients

- Prescreening clients by phone

- Preparing client materials

- Planning consultations

- Driving to appointments

- Meeting with clients for consultation

- Writing work agreements/contracts

- Billing clients

- Paid classes or seminars you give

Performing Organizing Services

- Onsite organizing at homes or offices

- Planning how best to organize

- Shopping for products clients need

- Consulting with clients by phone

Operational Tasks

- Business planning

- Filing

- Bookkeeping

- Budgeting/financial planning

- Banking

How does all this fit into a daily schedule? This is really up to you, but remember that you need to find the right mix of time spent in the office and out on the job.

Professional organizer Brenda Clements told us she prefers to designate one day a week for operational tasks, and uses the other days for client appointments and sales and marketing. Because she specializes in relocation organizing for seniors, she also works some weekends and evenings. Some professional organizers do their office operational tasks in the morning before they visit clients, or at the end of each day.

Consider the following when planning your work schedule:

- How many hours do you want to work a week? Some professional organizers work full and packed schedules each week; others do it as a part-time venture.

- What is the best time for you to get work done in your home office? As mentioned, you may choose to have your office hours when the other members of your family are at work and school.

- When do your clients like to schedule appointments? Depending on what your specialty is you may visit clients during the regular business day, at night or on the weekends, too.

- What other personal considerations affect your schedule? Do you want to take Fridays off to be with your kids? Are you taking continuing education courses? Are you working another job part time while you get this one going?

You can start using the scheduling forms for clients in Chapter 3 to prepare your own daily schedule. You can continue to change it and update it based on what you feel works best for you. You can plan your time using the devices we reviewed in that chapter as well, including planner calendars, PDAs with scheduling software, or computer-based scheduling software like Microsoft Outlook. It doesn't matter which one you use as long as you are comfortable with it, and it works for you.

4.3.2 Pricing Your Services

"I charge an hourly rate and they don't pay me until the job is done. I have never had a problem collecting payment [in] seven years."

— Brenda Clements, Professional Organizer

As a professional organizer you will have to determine what to charge for your organizing services, and how to structure your fees in a way that best compensates you for your work.

While some professional organizers charge as little as $20 per hour, in a NAPO survey of professional organizers, most charged what worked out to anywhere between $40 and $200 per hour. On her website OnlineOrganizing.com, professional organizer Ramona Creel adds that although this is an accurate range, the average hourly rate for a professional organizer in the United States is between $45 and $65 an hour.

Of course, the price you charge will be individual to your location, your market, and your financial goals, as well as the project and the type of organizing being done, as explained in the following section on factors in pricing.

Remember that whatever you set your fees at, you should believe in the value of your services. When you do an initial consultation, remind clients that although there is a fee for your services, you will be saving them time and making them more productive, both of which have a significant value. You will likely be saving them more money in the long run than you charge.

Factors in Pricing

When setting your prices for your services and products, consider the difference between the price you charge and the total cost to you to provide it. This difference determines your profit (or loss).

Remember that costs are not always simple and straight-forward. Direct costs, or variable costs, are costs associated with the product itself, while fixed costs are the overhead costs to run your business. You need to consider both to determine your full costs to cover (many people forget to factor in the overhead).

The "break-even point" is the point where your income from sales equals your total costs. Selling more than your break-even point creates a profit; selling less than your break-even point creates a loss. So here is the goal: sell enough services and products at a price that will cover your total costs and make a profit.

Your pricing must also reflect what the market will bear—or what clients are willing to pay. This may be affected by the perceived value of your service or product, and what price potential clients are paying for similar services elsewhere. It may also be influenced by whether your market is residential or corporate. Can you compete with every other professional organizer? No, and you don't want to. What you do want to do is determine what a fair price is in your specialty and your geographical area.

Finally, you need to consider how much money you want to make annually, and how many billable hours will it take you to meet this goal. For example, if you want to make $30,000 per year to start, but only want to work 20 hours a week, you'll need to charge a minimum of around $30 an hour. Keep in mind that there may also be weeks you don't make your 20 hours (holidays, slow times of the year) so you should factor that into your price too.

As you become more experienced and well known in your specialty you may decide to raise your prices. "Tweak" your prices and find the perfect range that not only brings you enough clients but pays you what you feel you are worth, while allowing you to make a healthy profit.

Pay Structures

Will you offer a free consultation, or charge for it? Will you charge for travel, or charge extra for working on weekends? Will you charge an hourly rate, a daily rate, or a flat fee for a certain service? Here is a look at the pros and cons of your options, so you can determine what type of fee structure is best for you.

Charge a Flat Fee

Some clients may want to know up front what the total cost will be for your services. These clients prefer to pay a "flat fee" rather than an hourly fee so they know the cost will not go above a certain amount.

With this pay structure, the organizer will quote a fee for a certain service, usually based on a site visit and initial consultation. So for example, if you visit a client's home and survey their garage, you might estimate it to take you about 10 hours to organize, and you know you want to make $60 an hour. Without divulging an hourly rate to the client, you would offer them a flat fee of $600 to organize their garage.

Many clients will be more comfortable with a flat fee, so they don't have to worry about how much a project is going to cost. You may get more clients who instantly agree to get the work done if you offer this "cards on the table" structure. The disadvantage to you is that, if the project takes longer than anticipated, you may be working for less than you would prefer. Of course the flip side is that you might finish earlier than you thought and make a better hourly rate.

Also, if the client insists on revisions, or requests changes after you have finished the project, they will likely expect you to make changes until they are satisfied at no cost beyond your quoted fee. Of course, this type of client is not the norm, but to protect yourself you may want to set a maximum of hours your flat fee covers, or bill reorganization over-and-above the flat fee.

The key to cost-effectively offering a flat fee is being confident in your estimates. If you are a beginning organizer, you may want to do a few projects on an hourly basis until you start to get a feel for the complexity each project offers, as well develop a trustworthy intuition as to what the client will want.

Offer a Price Range Per Service

Another "flat-rate" type option is to offer a general price range based on the type of organizing you will be doing. For example, if your specialty is closets, you can assume that there can really only be so much involved in organizing such a small space. You could set a price range from $200 - $600 (plus product purchases) based on small, medium and large square footages.

Once again, this type of pricing arrangement makes the client feel more comfortable agreeing to your services—providing an up-front price range clients can consider can help people see if they are in the right ballpark in terms of what they want to spend.

Some potential disadvantages are that you are offering a price without seeing the scope of the work involved, and that you might scare off people who think they can't afford your services, without being able to explain them in person or negotiate.

Charge an Hourly or Daily Rate

In this scenario, you charge your client a certain dollar amount for each hour or portion of an hour you work for them. For example, you might charge your clients $60 an hour for the 12.5 hours you spend with them, and then give them a bill for $750 when the project is complete.

For many beginning organizers, an hourly rate is the easiest route to go. When you are first starting out, it may be difficult to estimate how long a project will take you. If you try to use other pay structures right away, it may be a while before you can accurately judge the scope of a project—which can be either good or bad. You may also find some clients might shy away from agreeing to an hourly rate, unless you set it fairly low, or put a cap on how many hours you may bill for.

You do not have to start at $20 per hour. In fact, depending on the type of clients you want to work with, you may want to charge a higher fee (such as $50 per hour) because it may actually make some clients more likely to work with you. In particular, many corporate clients are likely to believe "you get what you pay for" so they may assume an organizer who charges $50 per hour is more experienced or will do a better job than one who charges $20 per hour.

You can also offer different hourly rates based on the type of service you are providing. For example, your rate for doing a needs-assessment might be $40 an hour, while your actual project fee might be $60 an hour. Or you might have a rate of $50 an hour for projects where you give advice, and $75 an hour when you work hands-on.

If you offer emergency organizing services, you can factor in a rush fee as well, that might be something like one-and-a-half times your regular rate. Depending on their specialty and/or availability, some organizers will also charge a premium rate for working evenings or weekends, if that is not part of their regular service.

If you decide to charge for travel time to and from a location, a standard rule of thumb is to charge only a portion of your hourly working rate—often, about half. If the site is quite far, you may also want to set a minimum number of hours you will bill per day—usually about 4 or 5—to justify your time getting there.

For larger projects, seminars, or speaking engagements, you can also set a daily rate, and set a minimum number of days, especially if you are traveling out of state. You can base this rate on the project, and get the details in writing in advance.

Offer a Free Initial Consultation

As mentioned earlier, many professional organizers choose to offer a free initial consultation, for either a half hour or a full hour. In such cases, this first meeting is simply an opportunity to learn more about what the clients need and explain how your services can benefit them. You can choose to bill for this initial consultation if you wish, but a good number of professional organizers feel that presenting their services face-to-face is key to making sales.

If you balk at the idea of offering your time and ideas for free, one solution is to bill your hourly rate (or half your hourly rate) for consultation, and offer that amount as a credit towards a purchase of the organizing service. Even if they choose not to have you do work for them, you will still be compensated for your time.

Charge for Organizing Products

When you help your clients get organized, you will likely be suggesting certain products they will need to get organized. Ideally the client will pay for all purchases themselves, or else you may end up out of pocket or items you can't use. If you do decide to pay for smaller purchases for your client, you can either charge clients exactly what you paid for the items, or else charge a small commission or finder's fee. Chapter 3 has more information on where to find organizing products for your clients.

Your Rate Sheet

You should be ready to present pricing information to clients in consultation appointments. Just like anything else consumers buy, people want to see that there are no hidden charges and that terms are spelled out. If you wish, you can prepare a rate sheet that includes your hourly rate or price ranges and, if you will set a minimum of hours, what that amount is.

Where and how you should present your pricing information is sometimes a judgment call. You don't want clients to think your prices are set in stone (unless they are) and you don't want to scare away clients with dollar figures. Some professional organizers don't put pricing information on a brochure either, because they like to determine the cost based on the job itself.

Sample Rate Sheet

Pro Organizing Services
1234 Orderly Boulevard
Tidy Town, TN 54321
(111) 555-1234

Organizing Service Pricing

Service	Rate
Initial Consultation (1 hour)	**Free!**
Needs Consultation	$40 per hour
Organizing Services	$60 per hour
Rush Services	$80 per hour
Special Services	As agreed with client
Travel (if more than 15 miles)	$20 per hour
Organizing Products	5% over purchase price

There is a 4-hour daily booking minimum for Organizing Services. Payment is due every 10 hours of service, or on completion of project. A 20% deposit is required at time of booking. We look forward to meeting your organizing needs!

Getting Paid

Most professional organizers who were interviewed for this book said they charge an hourly rate that clients pay by check at the end of each appointment.

Some professional organizers who work for business clients invoice their clients. Corporate clients are usually invoiced at the end of each project, or they can be invoiced monthly if a project is ongoing. A challenge with invoicing on a monthly basis is that corporations normally expect at least 30 days to pay, and some wait 60 or 90 days before putting a check in the mail.

Fortunately, you do not have to wait until the end of a project to start getting paid. During your initial consultation, if the client wants to go ahead, you can ask the client for a retainer (a deposit) for work you will be doing. Retainers for service businesses range anywhere from 20 to 50 percent of what the anticipated total cost of the project will be.

TIP: To protect yourself, buy any organizing supplies for a client only after you receive a deposit from that client.

When you give the client an invoice, detail the items you purchased, prices and taxes, and your commission, if any. Make sure to provide the client with receipts, as some items may be a tax write-off for them.

Your invoice should be on your letterhead and include the following. (See the next page for a sample invoice. Another sample is included on the CD-ROM.)

- The client name and contact information

- The date of the invoice

- A purchase order number (if the client gave you one)

- Services you provided

- Any taxes payable

- Any expenses you have paid (also known as disbursements)

- The total amount due

- Terms of payment (e.g. "Payable upon receipt" or "Payable within 30 days")

4.3.3 Client Contracts

A contract can prevent misunderstandings and help ensure you get paid. Your contract should spell out what services you will provide for the client, when you will provide them (the dates between which or by which your services are to be completed), as well as when and how you are to be paid. The contract should also include your company name and address, as well as the contact name, company name (if applicable) and address of your client.

Sample Invoice

Pro Organizing Services
1234 Orderly Boulevard
Tidy Town, TN 54321
(111) 555-1234

INVOICE

DATE: November 5, 2007

TO: Carla Client
XYZ Corporation
123 Main Street
Sunnyday, CA 90211

RE: **Professional Organizing Services**

Project Fee (as per contract of Sept. 7, 2007)	$2,000.00
Tax on Project Fee *(insert your own tax rate)*	200.00
Expenses (receipts enclosed) *(list each item purchased and the cost)*	195.23
TOTAL	2,395.23
Less: Deposit	(1,000.00)
Total – Please pay this amount	**$1,395.23**

Terms: Payable upon receipt.
Thank you for your business.

On the pages that follow you will find two sample contracts. The first is a sample "engagement letter" you might use with an individual client. You could ask your clients to sign it at your initial meeting, or have them return it to you later.

The second sample is a "services agreement" which you could adapt for use with a corporate client. It covers a number of additional areas, such as a liability disclaimer so that you cannot be held responsible for defects in items you buy or services you subcontract for your clients.

You can adapt these contracts to fit your needs. Before using any contract, make sure you have it reviewed by your lawyer.

Sample Engagement Letter

Pro Organizing Services
1234 Orderly Boulevard
Tidy Town, TN 54321
(111) 555-1234

[Insert name of Client]
[Insert address of Client]

[Date]

Dear [Name of client],

As promised, I have set out below a description of the services that [your name/company] will provide to you.

I will provide the following services:
[Insert description of the services]

My fee for the services performed will be as follows:
[Insert rates, amount of deposit, etc.]

If you agree that the foregoing fairly sets out your understanding of our agreement, please sign a copy of this letter in the space indicated below, and return it to me at [insert address, fax number or e-mail address].

Yours sincerely,

[Name]

Agreed and Accepted:

_____
[Insert name of client]

_____
Date

Standard Services Agreement

THIS AGREEMENT is made this [date] day of [month], 20__.

BETWEEN
[insert name of your client] (the "Client"), and [insert your name or your company's name] (the "Professional Organizer"), collectively referred to as the "Parties."

1.1 Services

The Professional Organizer shall provide the following services ("Services") to the Client in accordance with the terms and conditions of this Agreement: [Insert a description of the services here].

1.2 Delivery of the Services

• Start date: The Professional Organizer shall commence the provision of the Services on [insert date here].

• Completion date: The Professional Organizer shall [complete/cease to provide] the Services [by/on] [insert date here] ("Completion Date").

• Key dates: The Professional Organizer agrees to provide the following parts of the Services at the specific dates set out below: [insert dates for specific activities].

1.3 Site

The Professional Organizer shall provide the Services at the following site(s): [insert details here if applicable, such as client's home, client's office, etc.]

1.4 Fees

As consideration for the provision of the Services by the Professional Organizer, the fees for the provision of the Services are [insert fees here] ("Fees").

The Client [shall/shall not] pay for the Professional Organizer's out-of-pocket expenses comprising [insert here, if agreed].

1.5 Payment

The Client agrees to pay the Fees to the Professional Organizer on the following dates: [also specify whether the price will be paid in one payment, in installments or upon completion of specific milestones].

The Professional Organizer shall invoice the Client for the Services that it has provided to the Client [monthly/weekly/after the Completion Date]. The Client shall pay such invoices [upon receipt /within 30 days of receipt] from the Professional Organizer.

Any charges payable under this Agreement are exclusive of any applicable taxes, duties, or other fees charged by a government body and such shall be payable by the Client to the Professional Organizer in addition to all other charges payable hereunder.

1.6 Warranty

The Professional Organizer represents and warrants that [she/he] will perform the Services with reasonable skill and care.

1.7 Limitation of Liability

Subject to the Client's obligation to pay the Fees to the Professional Organizer, either Party's liability arising directly out of its obligations under this Agreement and every applicable part of it shall be limited in aggregate to the Fees. The Professional Organizer assumes no liability due to the quality of items or services purchased for the Client.

1.8 Term and Termination

This Agreement shall be effective on the date hereof and shall continue until the completion date stated in section 1.2 unless terminated sooner. If the Client terminates this agreement for any reason before the scheduled completion date, the Client will reimburse the Professional Organizer for all outstanding fees and out-of-pocket expenses.

1.9 Relationship of the Parties

The Parties acknowledge and agree that the Services performed by the Professional Organizer, its employees, sub-contractors, or agents shall be as an independent contractor and that nothing in this Agreement shall be deemed to constitute a partnership, joint venture, or otherwise between the parties.

1.10 Confidentiality

Neither Party will disclose any information of the other which comes into their possession under or in relation to this Agreement and which is of a confidential nature.

1.11 Miscellaneous

The failure of either Party to enforce its rights under this Agreement at any time for any period shall not be construed as a waiver of such rights.

If any part, term or provision of this Agreement is held to be illegal or unenforceable neither the validity or enforceability of the remainder of this Agreement shall be affected.

This Agreement constitutes the entire understanding between the Parties and supersedes all prior representations, negotiations or understandings.

Neither Party shall be liable for failure to perform any obligation under this Agreement if the failure is caused by any circumstances beyond its reasonable control, including but not limited to acts of God, war, or industrial dispute.

This Agreement shall be governed by the laws of the jurisdiction in which the Professional Organizer is located.

Agreed by the Parties hereto:

SIGNED by _____

on behalf of _____
                          [the Client]
SIGNED by _____

on behalf of _____
                    [the Professional Organizer]

4.3.4 Bookkeeping

Keeping your books essentially means that you know how much money you have coming in, and you know how much money you have going out. It really is that simple. Even if you didn't excel in mathematics and you have never taken an accounting class, there are a number of excellent accounting and business software programs available to help you set up your books simply — without doing all the "brain time" yourself.

Many small business owners take charge of day-to-day accounting and leave the monthly or yearly reports to an accountant. To do this you will need to enter information into the computer program (or by hand in a ledger) on a frequent basis. Leaving it all to the day before the accountant comes is never a good thing, so make time for bookkeeping in your week.

What You Should Know

Ideally you should know enough about your business' books to be able to do them yourself if you need to, and certainly to be able to check the accuracy and honesty of those whom you employ. Experts agree that one of the biggest mistakes new business owners make is that they simply don't understand what is happening with their business financially.

> **TIP:** Make sure that you spend some time looking at accounting software and finding one that does what you need, but isn't so complicated that you need to be a CPA to understand it.

You should understand how much money you owe, and how much money is owed to you. Particularly if you sell products as well as services, you should know how much money you are taking in per day. You should also be able to get a sense of where you are financially, and where you need to be to be successful.

If this is foreign territory to you, get a beginning accounting book and read over the key concepts, or consider taking a beginning accounting class at a local community college. Even a little bit of knowledge can be a fantastic tool for organizers. Here are some helpful definitions to get you on the right track.

Accounts Payable/Receivable

Accounts payable reports will tell you what bills you owe and when they are due. You have to be able to pay all your incoming bills and still have enough money for the other things you need to purchase for your business. An accounts payable report will help you to schedule when you will pay your bills, and will help you to make sure they are all paid on time.

Accounts receivable reports are the monies that are owed to you. This report will understandably be more complicated if you accept credit cards or if you sell products over the Internet.

Balance Sheet

A balance sheet is the quickest way to see how your business is doing at a glance. It shows you what you own and what you owe. In other words, it is a "balance" of your assets and your liabilities. When your assets exceed your liabilities, you've got equity. Balance sheets are used for a momentary snapshot, and the information compiled in them may change daily.

Cash Flow Statement

With a cash flow statement you will be able to see where the cash is in your business and how you are paying for things. They help you to ensure that you are not putting out more than you can handle based on what is coming in, and that you are spending money in appropriate ratios.

Daily/Weekly Sales Report

Ideally you will make money every day, or at least every week. You may get cash, take credit cards or debit cards, and you may accept checks. A daily or weekly sales report logs all of this information into the appropriate categories. Some professional organizers do their DSR by hand using a form. Look for accounting software that allows you to enter this information.

Income/Profit and Loss Statement

Your income statement, or profit and loss statement, will tell you how much money you have in expenses and how much money you have in revenue. It will help you keep tabs on your costs, your profit margin, and your operating expenses. In the end, this statement will tell you how much money your business is making or what is commonly referred to as the "bottom line."

4.3.5 Hiring Staff

According to NAPO president Barry Izsak, there are numerous multi-person organizing companies springing up across the U.S. Even if you start small, there is a likelihood that someday you may wish to hire people to work for you. If you do, you will have to adhere to the employment laws that other businesses do.

To find qualified staff to work with you, you can place an ad, or, better yet, use your superior networking skills and spread the word within the professional organizing industry that you are looking to hire some help. But before you decide to hire anyone, make sure you consider the real costs of hiring.

Pay Scale

How much will you pay your new employee(s)? What is the minimum wage in your area? Also, what other professional organizers are paying their employees has bearing on what you will pay. Remember that making a pay rate too low may cause employee turnover, which in turn costs you money, especially if you have to hire often.

Employer Contributions

When you determine payroll costs you must add in the matched employer contributions for federal programs and worker's compensation insurance costs. For example, the current percentage of employer-matched contribution for social security and Medicare is 7.65% of individual gross wages.

Overtime Wages

If your employees are considered nonexempt employees, they are eligible to receive overtime wages. Take a good look at what overtime wages will cost your business and if it makes sense to hire an extra employee instead.

Workers' Compensation

The cost of Workers' Compensation insurance is based on rates determined by industry classification.

Other Costs

You will need to determine costs for unemployment insurance, paid vacations, sick days, holidays or bonuses for employees, and medical benefits. Also you must determine if you will set up an employee commission structure or offer additional compensation for employees on jury duty. Some of these are mandatory, and others will be based on your personal decision about what will work best for your budget and business.

Complying with Law

The U.S. and Canadian governments have many laws that protect workers in the workplace. It is important to be aware of these laws and to make sure that your business abides by them. Also, ensuring compliance with all workplace laws will help you protect your business from the occasional disgruntled employee.

Make sure to check how these laws affect your business and how you can abide by them. There are a number of resources in section 4.1 that can provide you with information about workplace laws.

5. Marketing and Sales

There are two things that all successful professional organizers are experts at. Naturally, the first is their skill as organizers, but second, and just as important, is their ability to market that skill to clients. This chapter of the guide will teach you unique ways of attracting clients to your business, and then techniques for convincing these potential clients to use your services.

5.1 Your Marketing Plan

Part of writing your business plan will involve developing a marketing plan that will outline who your target market is, and how you plan to reach them. This section will give you parameters to define your target market and go over some marketing tools you'll want to have on hand before you start in on the techniques in the following section.

5.1.1 Choosing a Target Market

To begin developing your marketing plan, consider the answers to these questions:

- What is your product?

- Who are your customers?

- Who is your competition?

- What is your niche?

Your Product

Your product is, simply put, what you sell. Professional organizers sell a variety of different things. Some are tangible, but most are what are known in sales as intangible. Intangible products are often harder to describe because you can't see them or touch them. This is why it is imperative that you can express it clearly and succinctly to clients.

Professional organizers might sell advice and expert knowledge — like consultation and consulting time as well as classes, seminars, and public appearances; services, like working in clients' homes or offices doing the action it takes to get the space organized; and products like books, articles, and organizing equipment.

Write a description of each of the services or products you plan to sell. This description will later be of use to you as you write your brochures and website material.

Your Customers

Your business needs clients to be a success. So who are these people? Determining who they are specifically is the act of targeting your market. Think about your services and products. Who will want them? Consider the part of the market you will go after — this is your *market segment*.

For example, if you decide to sell residential services, your market will be people with living spaces — which is a pretty giant segment of the market. To determine the specific segment that you want to target, think about the segment of the market that will both want what you sell, and that you will most enjoy working with.

Perhaps you will target young professionals without children, or parents, or maybe you will choose retirees. It's completely up to you to determine your target market — and you can change it or refine it as your business grows and changes. Write a description of who your clients are. Consider these questions:

- Who are your clients?
- Where do your clients live?
- What is their income level?
- What do they do for a living?
- What is their age range?
- What do they do in their fun and leisure time?

This information will help you figure out how to market your product to them successfully. Once you know who your clients are you can figure out how to reach them.

> **TIP:** You can get demographic information about your area from your local newspaper. Newspapers prepare demographic information about their customers and give this to potential business advertisers.

Your Competition

It is helpful to determine who your competition is and how they are selling their products and services to the marketplace. This will allow you to present your products and services in a unique way, keep aware of market standards like pricing and services that other organizers offer, and be aware of how your competition pursues business and who their clients are.

Figure out who will compete with you, and then describe their businesses in your marketing plan. You might find competition in your surrounding physical area or your specific industry niche or specialty. For example, a professional organizer who sells her services over the Internet is in direct competition with all of the other organizers who do, too, regardless of where they live.

The more you know about your competition the easier it will be to create a unique set of products and services to offer clients. The more you know the better informed your marketing decisions will be.

Your Niche

Your niche is the place you fit into the industry. Knowing your niche, or specialty, will help you to determine your market and determine what you sell, too. When a professional organizer talks about being a specialist, it means he or she has determined their own niche in the marketplace. To review niches or specialties in professional organizing, you can reread section 2.2.4 in Chapter 2.

Consider these questions to describe your business' niche:

- What role does your business play in the industry?

- What is the one thing that you do the best?

- What do you want to be known for?

5.1.2 Marketing Tools

There are a variety of marketing tools that will give your clients or potential clients something to look at, to review, and will add a sense of legitimacy to your business — they are marketing tools.

People are tactile. They want information that they can hold in their own hands and take away from a meeting and read at their leisure. Tangible things let them know that your business is reputable, credible, and trustworthy. Clients need to feel confident in you to make a buying decision.

Also, you can use your materials as visual aids during a client consultation. Just point at something and give a potential client the opportunity to read it and hear you at the same time. This is helpful for some clients who like to learn using written information.

Business Cards

"I have a four-color two-sided business card with my photograph on it… I realize that people like to see who is going to come into their home ahead of time. With my picture on my card, clients can identify me before I walk into their homes."

— Chris McKenry, Professional Organizer

Your business card should be something you are proud of and that you feel represents you well. It doesn't have to be wildly expensive, either. Your business card should include your name and title, your business address (see below), your business and cell phone number, your website, your email address, and some indication of what you do. Many cards will also include a logo or slogan.

Most experts will advise that, for safety and privacy reasons, you don't use your home address on your business card, even if you work from home. Because people don't like to do business with those who do not have a physical address, often the best way to go is to rent a personal mailbox from a company like Mail Boxes Etc. You may be required to put "PMB" on your business card to indicate it is a personal mailbox.

The business cards you select will help convey the image of your company, so give some thought to what you want. Your card should say enough about you to give people a sense of what you can do for them. Include your specializations, your website address so they can get more information, and consider a special offer, such as: "Call today for a free consultation."

Pass your business cards out whenever it is appropriate. Give them to your friends, your relatives, people you meet at social functions, the people behind the counter at your local coffee shop, your dentist, your mail carrier. Mention that you are a professional organizer when handing out your card, so that people will look at it later and make the connection. When you send letters to people, stick a business card in the envelope. Make sure that you carry at least three or four business cards in your wallet or purse at all times.

If your start-up finances are limited, you might want to consider getting free business cards from VistaPrint. They offer color business cards on heavy paper stock, and a number of different designs are available. In return for the free cards (all you pay is shipping, which starts at around $5) they print their logo and "Business Cards are free at VistaPrint.com" on the back of the card near the bottom.

If you don't want anything printed on the back, you can get their premium cards for only $29.99 plus shipping, which is still a value price. Visit **www.vistaprint.com**.

Another company that offers quality business cards and stationery at reasonable prices is Design Your Own Card.com. The company offers templates, fonts, and logos to choose from and can have your business cards on your doorstep within a few days. The company's website is **www.designyourowncard.com**.

Brochures

A brochure should explain the finer points of your business when you are not there to do it yourself. It should be colorful enough to catch the attention of clients, but not too busy; professional, flawlessly proofed, informative, interesting, and memorable. It will include:

- Your company name and contact information

- An appropriate, attractive photo on the front panel

- A logo or slogan

- A list of your services

- An overview of your business

- A short bio and a picture of you

- Your association affiliations and their logos

- Some brief testimonials from clients or people you've worked with

- Anything else that you feel gives your business credibility

But what if you aren't a writer or you have never made your own brochure before? You can still put together a great brochure if you follow these steps.

Get Some Examples

Networking or attending a trade show are great ways to gather marketing materials to look at. You don't necessarily have to see the brochures of other professional organizers — any brochure that sells a service prepared by a self-employed or small business owner is a helpful thing for you to view.

Jot Down Your Ideas

These ideas can later be used to create a rough draft for your brochure. You can also use the work you did in Chapter 4 in which you brainstormed about and described your business to come up with your brochure ideas.

Write Your Bio

A bio is a short, biographical paragraph (or two) about you. It should include your name and company's name, and the area your business serves; your professional focus or specialty; your recent claims to fame; and products or services your business offers that are especially interesting. You can save this bio and use it with press releases, articles you write, and on your website.

To get a quick sense of how to write your business bio, take a look at the short bios of the professional organizers who were interviewed at the end of this guide.

Make a Rough Draft

You can make a rough draft with the information you have so far. One easy way to do this is with a pencil and a piece of paper. Just take a standard-sized piece of paper and fold it as your brochure will be folded. Most brochures are three-panel brochures, so fold your rough draft paper just as if you are folding a letter to place in an envelope. Sketch out how you want the information to appear.

Lay it Out

Now that you have a rough draft, you are ready to move to your computer. Some software programs like MS Works or MS Publisher have "wizard" features that allow you to move through pre-organized template steps and simply fill in your text and add pictures and logos. If you are new to desktop publishing, MS Works is a little easier to use, but has some limits to it as well.

If you don't think you can design this yourself, a printer should be able to put together what you have in mind, for an additional cost.

Print It

Bring your layout or your draft to a neighborhood printer for a quote, or consider an online brochure-making website like the ones below. You will need to choose a type of paper, how many colors you want, and an overall size. Don't make your brochure so wide that it won't fit in a normal envelope, or you will pay extra in postage.

If you have a good quality printer at home you can simply make prints at home, or try a place like Kinko's, but be aware that the quality may not project as professional an image as you would like. An average price range is about 10 cents to $1 per brochure.

- *Vista Print Brochures*
  www.vistaprint.ca/vp/ns/splash/splash_brochure.aspx

- *My Brochure Maker — Sponsored by Hewlett Packard*
  www.mybrochuremaker.com/mybrochuremaker-fun.html

5.2 Marketing Techniques

No two businesses are ever going to market themselves exactly the same. You will use the information you have gathered about your target market to determine what mix of the following techniques are likely to work for you. Marketing is always a work in progress, so if certain techniques don't seem to be effective for you, you want to be open to changing them until you find you are generating leads and results.

5.2.1 Networking

"When people ask me what I do, I am always available with business cards and explanations. I don't do any print advertising or television or anything like that. One hundred percent of my business comes from networking and word of mouth."

— Rozanne Hird, Professional Organizer

Networking is the fine art of opening up your mind and your mouth. You have to be open to new situations and the infinite possibilities that getting to know other people will provide you. You also have to be comfortable letting people know your professional mission on a daily basis, even in unexpected places. Networking is a superb source of information, business, knowledge, and opportunity.

Professional organizers spend a lot of their time finding networking organizations to be part of so they can speak to people who may need their services. Word of mouth advertising is free (with the exception of fees associated with joining a group of any kind), and it allows professional organizers to pick and choose the groups of people they want to associate with and eventually have as clients.

So how do you do it? Well, if you think you have never networked, the fact is, you undoubtedly have. Anytime you have talked to someone and shared information that helped either one of you, you have networked. Here are a few techniques that anyone can use to network effectively anytime.

When and Where to Network

People who are really good at networking will tell you that they spend time finding the right places to network. They find business associations, clubs, charity and philanthropic organizations, and other groups where they go and spend time representing themselves and their businesses.

All great networkers know that you can network anywhere there are people to talk to. What about some of these excellent networking spots you may not have considered?

- Grocery store

- Airplane

- Library

- Waiting room

- In line

- At your child's school or sporting event

- With your neighbors

- With service people

- At church

- At the gym

Tips for Networking Success

Come Prepared...

Decide on a networking objective before you attend a networking event. Consider these sample objectives:

- I will talk to ten people

- I will get ten business cards

- I will give out ten business cards

- I will make three important connections that will help my business

...But Network When You Aren't Prepared!

If you can make a plan, and yet be flexible enough to know when to change gears, you can be open to all networking possibilities. Many great deals have been written on cocktail napkins. There are many instances when you haven't necessarily prepared to network, but suddenly you find yourself in a situation to connect. In this case, the number one rule is, speak up. Don't let a potential lead slip through your fingers.

Stay Focused...

Great networkers stay focused. They gently move conversations the way they want them to go. They keep in mind that they have an objective and they try, while being charming and positive and friendly, to meet their objectives. This takes a certain amount of concentration. So turn off your cell phone, and focus on the person you are connecting with and your objective. It is not only gracious, but also it helps you think clearly.

...But be Prepared to Shift Gears!

Here is a funny story about an unexpected networking gift:

> A woman named Jen was working recruiting people for her son's school carnival. She had a list of names and needed to stay focused to meet her goal of ten volunteers by the end of her calling session. As she finished a phone call and put her phone down, it instantly rang again — with a wrong number.

The lady on the other end of the phone was very pleasant and apologetic, and indicated she was looking for a business that Jen had some information about. Jen took the time to help this lady, which led into a brief conversation about Jen's carnival volunteer objective.

It turned out that the lady on the phone was in charge of her church's volunteer group and before she knew it, Jen had her ten volunteers — plus more. Jen turned a wrong number into an opportunity to meet her volunteer quota. She kept her mind open and was rewarded with networking success.

Naturally a combination of good sense and instinct will help you to weed through the unexpected situations that are just a waste of time, but keep an open mind.

The One-Minute Business Commercial

One popular networking technique is a quick, catchy and polished thirty second or one-minute speech in which you introduce yourself, briefly describe the most important services you provide, and end with a cute or catchy saying at the end. You can use it at NAPO meetings, at your Chamber of Commerce, or with any group in which you are asked to stand and share a bit about yourself.

Before you head out to network, try to prepare a one-minute commercial of your own. Introduce yourself, tell what you do and why it's helpful, and mention at least one unique service you offer. You can set up a problem, question, or emotional need, and then solve the problem or answer the question. End with a catchy slogan you devise. For example:

"Hi, my name is Tara Tidy, and I own Tidy Solutions, a professional organizing business serving both residential and corporate customers in the City of Clutter. Have you got more stuff than you can handle? Have you lost track of what you have? Is your mess making your life frustrating and unhappy? Tidy Solutions has an answer. I have created a four-point system that will take you from harried to happy in just four weeks. Tidy isn't just what your mom used to say, Tidy is the better way! Call me today — I'm Tara Tidy of Tidy Solutions."

Try developing your own one-minute commercial using the template below.

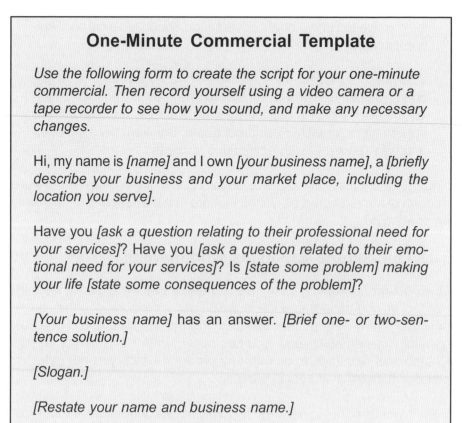

One-Minute Commercial Template

Use the following form to create the script for your one-minute commercial. Then record yourself using a video camera or a tape recorder to see how you sound, and make any necessary changes.

Hi, my name is *[name]* and I own *[your business name]*, a *[briefly describe your business and your market place, including the location you serve]*.

Have you *[ask a question relating to their professional need for your services]*? Have you *[ask a question related to their emotional need for your services]*? Is *[state some problem]* making your life *[state some consequences of the problem]*?

[Your business name] has an answer. *[Brief one- or two-sentence solution.]*

[Slogan.]

[Restate your name and business name.]

5.2.2 Get Media Publicity

The "media" are magazines, newspapers, radio, and television. When a business gets publicity in a magazine article, newspaper story, radio or television talk show, it can result in a tremendous amount of new business. Here are some ways to get publicity for your business.

Write a Press Release

Books, newspapers, magazines, e-zines, trade magazines, and newsletters are all excellent places to get attention for your organizing business. Getting your name and your advice into print – even if you are just briefly quoted – makes you an expert in the eyes of the reader.

In order to get someone to write about you in the media, you need to generate interest and excitement about your business. An effective way to spread the word about your organizing business is with a press release. A press release is a marketing tool that you give to the press.

In it you tell them about things that your company is doing that are new and exciting, or "newsworthy." They may print your press release verbatim, or call you for more information to write an article about you.

Your press release should be brief, informative, and include contact information for you and your business. As there is somewhat of a "standard" format to follow, you can use the websites and sample fictional release provided on the next few pages to guide you through writing your first release.

- *Guide to Writing Successful Press Releases*
  www.stetson.edu/~rhansen/prguide.html

- *Inside Secrets for Writing the Perfect Press Release*
  www.publicityinsider.com/release.asp

When to Send Out a Release

Any time your business does anything of note, you should write a press release. Many times businesses use press releases to let the press know what they are planning to do. If the press hears about what your company is planning to do ahead of time, and it is presented in a newsworthy manner, then you have a better chance of having a news item printed based on your press release.

One great way to get press for your business is to do newsworthy things. Get involved in your community. Join groups, associations, and clubs that are doing things in the public eye. Join charitable organizations as a representative of your business and do good works.

Each and every time you do something of note as a professional organizer — each time you speak, each time you get an award or give a class, or do anything else worthy of attention, write a press release and submit it to your press contacts.

Sample Press Release

FOR IMMEDIATE RELEASE

Author Grace Jasmine Presents Seminar on *How Your Mess is Making You Sick*, at Women's Conference.

Contact:

Grace Jasmine, President and Owner, Serenity Solutions
123 Good Karma Way #123, Calmington, CA 91234
(123) 555-1234

June 1, 2007

Local business owner and author Grace Jasmine will present her acclaimed seminar, "Get Organized and Get Well — How Your Mess Is Making You Sick!" at the 23rd annual International Women's Conference.

Ms. Jasmine, a professional organizer and owner of Serenity Solutions, recently made news as her latest book (published under the same name) hit the nonfiction bestseller list. She has just returned from the National Organization of Professional Organizers' annual conference where she led a two-day session on the relationship of illness to lack of organization.

Grace Jasmine's local professional organizing business, Serenity Solutions, has been on the map since 1998 when she realized that her life was completely out of control. As an author who had "hacked away" at more than 40 books, Jasmine one day woke up to the fact that she was swimming in paper, behind on her deadlines, and a literal and literary mess. What began as a catastrophe caused Jasmine to turn her organizational life around — which resulted in a dramatic upswing in her own physical health.

As Jasmine saw the changes in her own life she began to share her techniques and successes with clients around the globe, while writing her now best-selling book. Jasmine's claim is that anyone can go from sick and swamped to sound and systematic in just 12 weeks.

Ms. Jasmine will be one of several authors slated to discuss their new books as well as appear at a celebrity roundtable at the annual International Women's Conference at the Calmington Conference Center June 12-15, 2007. The conference will feature a women's topic tradeshow with more than 250 vendors from 35 countries worldwide.

For booking information, personal consulting and seminar details contact Grace Jasmine at (123) 555-1234. Information about the 23rd Annual International Women's Conference can be obtained by calling 1-800-FOR-GALS. Serenity Solutions can be visited on the Internet at www.serenitysolutions.com.

###

Attention-Getting Tips

Establish a Relationship With the Press

Get a copy of all the local newspapers in your area and read them — not only the business section, but also any section that you think your potential clients will read. A professional organizer who specializes in residential organizing will probably want to be mentioned in a different section of the paper than a business organizer will. Consider the arts and leisure section, or the home section too.

Read the feature stories and decide which writers you like the best. Contact these writers about doing a feature story on your business and send them a press release. You can call or email and introduce yourself and your business, briefly explain what is going on with your business that is new and exciting, and ask the writer to call you back once they receive the release.

Once you have made initial contact, send the press release, then call back to follow up and see if they are interested in writing about you.

Offer to Be Interviewed

Sometimes getting someone to interview you or do a feature story about your business is as easy as offering. Writers at newspapers are looking for stories. Let them know you are available to be interviewed. Sometimes just making people aware that you are willing to be interviewed is all it takes.

Look for Opportunities

Many professional organizers agree to be interviewed for radio programs; some even participate in local cable television shows. Look for ways to use these traditional forms of media in less traditional ways — and ways that aren't as expensive as purchasing ad, radio, or television time.

Get on Talk Shows

Another excellent way to get publicity for your business is to get interviewed on radio and television.

Phone local radio and TV shows to let them know you are available to provide advice to their viewers or listeners about how to get organized. You'll find some topic ideas in section 5.2.3.

Shows that might be appropriate include morning shows and afternoon talk shows. The person to contact is the producer of each show.

The producer will probably ask you to send them some information, so be prepared to email or fax a few paragraphs about yourself, along with a list of frequently asked questions. These are questions their audience would likely be interested in knowing the answer to. You can put any questions you like on the list, but chances are whatever you find people asking your advice about are questions that an audience would be interested in, as well.

Television is a visual medium, so you could propose a demonstration of organizing techniques in the TV studio. Another possibility is to have a camera follow you during an actual organizing job (set it up with a friend or get permission from a client) and show "before and after" shots.

5.2.3 Write a Column or Article

Getting your words in print is an amazing marketing tool. Professional organizers know that having their advice on organizing published gives them instant credibility. Here are two ways you can go from a professional organizer with good ideas to a professional organizer whose words are in print.

Write a Column

One of the best ways to establish yourself as an expert is to write a column for a newspaper, magazine, or newsletter. While it can be tough to break into large daily newspapers, there may be an opportunity to write a column for smaller newspapers or local magazines.

You could write on any topic related to organizing, or propose an "Ask the Professional Organizer" column where you would answer questions from readers. The length and frequency of your column will depend on the publication. You might produce a weekly 500-word column for a local newspaper, or a monthly 1,000-word column for a newsletter or magazine.

Make sure your column provides valuable information to the publication's readers. As with press releases, columns that sound like an ad for your services are not likely to get published.

Once you have written your first column, phone the editor to ask if they would be interested in seeing it. If so, they will probably ask you to email it. If they want to publish it, they may offer to pay you. However, even if they don't pay, you should consider letting them publish it in return for including a brief bio and your contact information at the end of the column.

Write an Article

Choose a Topic and Title

Yes, you want to write about organizing, but you have to have an angle. An angle is an approach you take to capture the reader's interest and get them to read your article. It doesn't have to be fancy — just catchy.

A reader should instantly get a sense about your article from the title and, at the very most, the first paragraph. A good article has a hook to draw the reader in. Consider these article titles. Notice how they do or do not get your attention.

"Yawn."	**"Wow!"**
How to Organize	How to Make Your Harried Home a Happy Haven
Getting Your Life In Order	Help, My Life Is Out of Order!
Fixing Organizing Problems	Organizing 101—Quick Fixes for Big Problems
Organize for Money	Clearing Clutter for Cash!

Work with a Formula

When you are just starting out writing articles, it may be useful to work with a set formula that you adapt to your topic. Here is a sample formula you can use to write a quick and effective article about organizing.

The Title	Use a catchy title that instantly informs your readers about the content of the article
Lead paragraph(s)	Explain the premise for the problem in an attention-grabbing way
Secondary paragraph(s)	Introduce the proposed solution
Concluding paragraph(s)	Give the solution
Conclusion	Sum everything up with an upbeat, positive and witty ending

TIP: One easy technique to write the concluding paragraphs is with a numbered or bulleted list explaining how to create something with simple, numbered instructions. You can study the example on the following pages for help.

Sample Short Article

Make a Mail Station in Less Than an Hour

You probably remember the Addams Family, a classic show from the 1960s that has spawned recent movies and cartoons of the same name. In this ghoulish family farce, "Thing" (a hand that resided in a box) was a "handy helper" around the house, doing what small tasks a hand could manage. When the mail arrived, Thing would pre-sort it, and hand over only the relevant mail.

We could all use a mail system that kept us organized, weeding out junk mail or documents we couldn't use. Unfortunately, Thing was the result of a TV writer's active imagination and not an item we can order for $19.95, so we continue to deal with the frustration of piles and piles of mail.

To compound the problem, junk mail now comes with your name and address on it, while bulky advertising supplements take up space. Mail gets scattered around the house, misplaced or lost, or even worse, bills are late and your credit rating is affected. Even your own credibility can be affected when important documents mailed to you are lost or misplaced.

Part of the problem stems from the fact that not everything that shows up in your mailbox warrants the same treatment. Your delivery person may toss any of the following into your box on a single day:

- Items that you want to deal with, but not immediately (e.g., subscription renewals, coupons)

- Bills that need paying within the month

- Correspondence that you want a chance to sit down and enjoy, or hold onto and reply

- Catalogs and magazines you want to read later

- Items you are undecided about (offers to clean your furnace, etc.)

What you need is a system to easily and quickly prioritize your mail, and the solution is a mail station you can make yourself. It's easy and inexpensive. Just read the directions below and you'll have you mail station ready to go in less than an hour! You'll need:

- A drawer or basket for storage
- A letter opener
- A wastepaper basket
- A shredder
- An accordion file
- Stamps
- Envelopes
- Address labels
- Pens
- Address book
- Checkbook
- Calculator

1. Find a space. Empty out a small drawer in an easily accessible area that will become your mail station. The drawer should be large enough to hold an accordion file and other mail implements. A kitchen or desk drawer works well, or if you have no drawer space, you can use a lidded container or small basket. The location must be near an outlet where you can plug in your shredder.

2. Arrange mail items. Place all of your mail necessities in the drawer.

3. Shred or recycle junk. Get rid of all junk mail and unnecessary mail. Shred anything with your name and address on it, and anything that is from a company with whom you do business.

---

4. Set up a system. Current mail can be placed in the accordion file according to categories like coupons, personal correspondence, and bills. You can file your bills according to company, or according the date that they must be dealt with. Remember if you are mailing bills, file a few days ahead to give it time to arrive by mail.

5. Using Your Mail Station. The next time you collect your mail, open your letters, purge your junk mail and unnecessary correspondence, shred secure information, and file your bills according to your "deal-with-by" date. Set a regular time each week to review the contents of your accordion file. Soon you will find that you are as organized as the Addams Family, and you hardly had to do — a Thing!

If you are still unable to get your ideas down on paper, you may be able to take a local or online writing class, like the ones from **WritingClasses. com**.

Sell it or Give it Away?

Once you have an article written, how do you get it into print? There are a number of ways; however, the most important rule to getting an article published is to submit it again and again until you find a publication that wants it.

Because your articles are generally written to promote your business, it is less crucial that you get paid when it is published. For this reason, you may want to speed up your chances of getting published by giving your articles to a publisher for free.

Find publications that you feel will reach your target audience and contact them letting them know you are interested in writing articles free of charge for their publication in exchange for a byline or bio that mentions your name, your business name, and your business contact information.

You can sell what you write — but it will likely take longer to get it into print. This doesn't mean you should be discouraged — even the best writers in the world have files and files full of rejection letters. Either way, make sure you indicate what your intention is when you submit your article.

Getting Published

There are a number of publications for writers that give contact and other relevant information for publishers of both magazines and books. The most well known is Writer's Market, available in bookstores and online at **www.writersmarket.com**.

While you can submit the entire article to some publications, others will request a query letter, particularly if you are hoping to sell the article. A query letter explains the importance of your topic and why you should write it for a publisher. It should be interesting, and succinct. A sample query letter is included on the CD-ROM.

5.2.4 Write a Tip Book or Booklet

A unique way that professional organizers get "published" in a hurry is to write their own books of organizing tips to sell or give away. Make a habit of writing down thoughts for organizing tips as they come to you, and in no time you will have enough for your own tip book.

If you want to start right away, you can review some of the concepts and techniques in Chapter 3 and pull them together in your own unique way. Each tip is usually only a few paragraphs long, and you can group them by category in your book. Here's an example:

Microwave Magic

Have you ever thought about how much time you stand in your kitchen waiting for the microwave to finish heating something? Waiting for that cup of tea or that frozen entrée can take three, four, even 10 minutes of your life each time you do it.

Let's say you use the microwave three times a day for five minutes — that's 5,475 minutes a year, or 91 hours! That is time you could devote to quick organizational routines without disrupting your schedule or devoting a lot of energy.

And it's amazing how much you can actually do in five minutes. You can pick up your living room, load your dishwasher, make a bed, empty the trash, or pay a bill. Just think how this painless time management technique will make your life so much easier!

There are a variety of ways you can publish your own tip book — and professional organizers have tip books that range from a pamphlet that is printed off on a laser printer to a book printed and bound by a professional printer. You can look at section 5.1.2 on writing a brochure for ideas on printing yourself or with a printer.

Don't worry if you aren't an author and you never plan to be one! Some professional organizers will sell you their tip books that you can use with clients. For example, Carol Halsey, owner of Business Organizing Solutions in Wilsonville, Oregon, has written a tip book that she often sells to other professional organizers around the United States and Canada.

Her tip book is sized so it can be placed in a regular-size envelope, and she produces it so that it can be customized as a sales tool for your business. When you purchase tip books in bulk her company will print your business name and logo on the cover. For more information, visit her website at **www.pilestofiles.com**.

5.2.5 Build a Website

Most professional organizers do not have a physical office location that clients visit. Because of this, a virtual destination is more than just your website, it is your company's "location." These days having a business website is practically as common – and as necessary – as having a business card, or a telephone number.

Having a good website can add credibility to your business, increase your clients, and give you another, sometimes very lucrative, way to sell your services and products. Even if you have little or no experience creating a website, you should make a commitment to have one for your business — even if it is a very simple one to begin.

What to Include

Your organizing business website will include some or all of the following:

- What your company does

- What areas you serve

- Who your typical clients are

- What your specialty is

- Contact information (email, phone, fax)

- Mailing address (personal mailbox or PO box)

- Organizing advice and tips

- Testimonials from satisfied clients

- Before-and-after pictures of organizing projects

- Any local or national association affiliations (NAPO, POC, Chamber of Commerce)

Your Domain Name

Most businesses try to have a website address that spells out their business name. This is called a domain name and you can purchase your domain name (or actually, "rent" it year by year) if someone else has not already chosen it. Most domain registration services cost about $20 a year. To find domain name registering options, search on the words "register domain name" in your web browser or visit **www.godaddy.com**.

Web Hosting

Once you have secured your domain name you need to get a web hosting service. The fee will vary based on the size and complexity of your website. Web hosting costs range from around $10 a year for a minimal one-page site, to several hundred dollars a month for a complex merchant website hosting.

Many website hosting companies feature built-in web utility software that is extremely easy to use, and designed for small business owners. One example is Yahoo.com's Small Business Merchant Solutions at **http:// smallbusiness.yahoo.com/ecommerce**.

5.2.6 Write an Email Newsletter

The use of email as a way to connect with clients is something that has become a standard practice with many business owners, and professional organizers are no exception. They use email to connect with their potential clients and sales leads, as well as to stay connected to those who are already clients to secure repeat and referral business.

One way to use email to your advantage is to write and send your own monthly email newsletter. An email newsletter can help you:

- Connect with potential clients and existing clients

- "Publish" your organizing articles and tips

- Make clients aware of upcoming events and promotions

- Keep your business name out there

- Generate interest in the success of your business

How to Create Your Newsletter

There are a variety of ways to produce an email newsletter. For example, Constant Contact is a website where you can create your email newsletter online. Visit **www.constantcontact.com**.

Some professional organizers use a text-only method. If you do it this way you can create the newsletter document in MS Word or any other word processing program, and send it out to your clients.

Remember that the overall look and presentation of your newsletter may be the first information that a potential client receives about your business. The more professional and eye-catching and effective it is, the more business it will generate for you. Even a short night class in desktop publishing should give you the skills to lay out a newsletter for your clients and clients-to-be.

On the next few pages is a sample newsletter, provided by Chris McKenry of Get It Together LA!

🖨 Print

Click Here If you wish to be removed from this e-mail list. Thank you.

Chris McKenry's

Organizing

Tips **Get It Together LA!**

Professional Organizing for the Home, Office, and Your Better Living

Spring Cleaning Month

Volume 2 - Number 5 May 2004

Organizing Tips in this issue

- **MAY DAY! Organizing This Spring**
- In the Kitchen...
- Organize Your Time
- Get Your Garage Together!
- Get It Together LA! Workshops Scheduled In June

In the Kitchen...

Empty your refrigerator completely. For any spills, such as ketchup on shelves, use a credit card to scrap off access then clean with soap and water. When restocking your fridge, place a new thermometer inside to be sure the temperature stays below 40 degrees. This will keep food bacteria from growing.

Organize your refrigerator and have zones for the different foods. Keep sandwich foods together. Meats and eggs should be in airtight containers -again preventing the spread of bacteria.

In your lower cabinets, remove everything so the shelves can be cleaned. Insert plastic shelf liner to protect the cabinets and make it easier to clean. For those bottom shelves, if you do not have roll-out selves this would be an excellent time to install. Roll- outs make it much easier to have access to those hard to reach areas and are available at most home stores.

Click here for printable grocery list »

Organize Your Time

Time is an important element to include in the organizing process. If there are never enough hours in your day, examine how your time is spent.

MAY DAY! Organizing This Spring

Is Spring Cleaning on your mind? When you look at your home are you thinking "May Day, May Day"! Think of "May Day's" as new start at organizing, or your clutter distress call.

Add simple organizing ideas to this year's spring cleaning and gain an extra hour each day. Since most of us spend up to an hour a day looking for what is needed, you could actually give yourself several extra weeks a year by being organized.

5/11/2004

Chart out each hour of the day including the activities performed. Then determine if there are more productive hours than others. Is it possible to get gas, go to the grocery and the bank all in the same trip?

During those hectic days take the extra time to put things away. You may think you are wasting time, but consider how much time are you loosing looking through your all that clutter.

Make Life Easy, Get Organized, Get It Together LA! »

Get Your Garage Together!

 From organizing to storage design to providing containers, Get It Together LA is YOUR one stop for EVERYTHING needed to get organized. We make the most of your wall space by installing vertical storage designed for your needs. Then zones are identified for the different tasks to be performed in your garage.

Containers are available in a wide variety of styles. Whether boxes or totes are used, all containers are clearly labeled for easy identification.

A garage O-Tip for You - A Polaroid picture of the contents of a container makes a great label.

For the best call 323-525-0678, or click here. »

Get It Together LA! Workshops Scheduled In June

Chris McKenry has two educational opportunities scheduled in June. This busy organizer and popular speaker enjoys sharing with others.

Small Business Week Event - "Networking: The Game Plan for Success" - Need to increase your networking skills? Join Chris McKenry and Maxine Tatlonghari on June 7 as they repeat this popular course for the fourth time since initiating one year ago. This event is sponsored by the West Hollywood Chamber of Commerce and will be held at Plummer Park, Room 2 from 6:00 - 8:00 pm. Contact the Chamber for registration information at 323-650-2688.

Schedule one room a day and thoroughly clean every cabinet and storage area. Throw out what you no longer need or use or make a donation to your favorite charity.

Stay focused on that room for the day. Do not get distracted with other parts of the home or office. Moving piles from one area to another accomplishes nothing. Take a short break every couple of hours so not to wear yourself out. Soon you will be enjoying extra time this summer.

For help with your Spring Organizing call 323-525-0678 or click here

Quick Links...

Get It Together LA!

Organized Living

Closets from Get It Together LA!

Make Life Easy, Get Organized

What clients have to say...

West Hollywood Chamber of Commerce

Join our mailing list!

5/11/2004

Home Organizing Event - "Get Your Clothes Together Seminar" - Ready for a new wardrobe? The possibilities are endless when all your clothes are in sight. By taking the time to go through your closet and drawers, you would be amazed at the outfits you already have. Organized Living, in Los Angeles, is the site of this workshop on June 24, at 6 pm.

enter email

Join

To schedule Chris McKenry for your next meeting, or for information on these events please call 1-866-226-3237, or click here »

email: chris@getittogetherla.com
voice: 323-571-2134, for outside California 866-226-3237
web: http://www.GetItTogetherLA.com

Get It Together LA! • 6230 Wilshire Blvd., Suite 1143 • Los Angeles • CA • 90048

Forward email

☒ SafeUnsubscribe™

This email was sent to chris@getittogetherla.com, by Get It Together LA!.
Update your profile |Instant removal with SafeUnsubscribe™ | Privacy Policy.

Powered by

Constant Contact
TRY IT FREE

What makes this a great email newsletter? Consider these reasons, and the impressions they convey:

- It provides easy-to read contact information *(call now!)*

- It includes several links to his website *(read more about his services!)*

- It includes links to customer testimonials *(you can trust him!)*

- It has original content related to his specialty *(he is helpful!)*

- It includes relevant links *(he goes the extra mile!)*

- It gives information about classes and speaking engagements that Chris is facilitating and/or presenting *(he is a good teacher!)*

- It makes it simple to join the mailing list *(he can simplify your life too!)*

5.2.7 Present Speeches, Classes, or Seminars

Giving Speeches

Speeches provide a free forum for professional organizers. It lets audience members get a sense of who you are and what you do, making them much more likely to hire you.

Professional organizers can speak to just about any group: churches, women's clubs, businesses, expos, fairs, nonprofit organizations, seniors' groups — anywhere people gather will become a place you can spread the word about organization.

Many associations hold monthly breakfast or luncheon meetings and need speakers to present keynote talks (about 10 to 20 minutes). Some of the groups you might consider speaking to include:

- Lions Clubs International
  www.lionsclubs.org

- Kiwanis
  www.kiwanis.org

- Rotary International
  www.rotary.org

- National Association of Women Business Owners
  www.nawbo.org

- General Federation Of Women's Clubs
  www.gfwc.org/about_us.jsp

Go online to research both the national organizations and the local chapters. You can also ask friends and acquaintances if they belong to any groups that have presentations from speakers. Contact people in local chapters who are in charge of programs and let them know that you are available to speak on getting organized. List one or more topics that their members are likely to be interested in learning about.

> **TIP:** The topics and titles of articles in section 5.2.3 also make excellent topics and titles for speeches and seminars.

While you probably will not be paid for your presentations, it can be an excellent opportunity to promote your business. Your company name may be published in the organization's newsletter, it will be mentioned by the person who introduces you, you can distribute business cards and brochures, and you can mingle with attendees before and after your presentation. If you give a good talk and offer useful advice, you will be seen as an expert. As long as there are people in the audience who need organizing services, this can be an excellent way to attract clients.

For organizers promoting their products as well as their services, their speaking engagements always have a table of their products displayed and someone to help them with the cash register. If you have created a book – even a small tip book – you will see that people who just enjoyed your talk will want to walk away from the experience with a purchase.

Teach a Class

Teaching a class can be a great way to earn extra money, establish your reputation, and meet prospective clients. You don't need a degree to teach adults — just lots of enthusiasm and knowledge.

Professional organizers are natural teachers, and teaching a class allows potential clients attending your class to get to know you and your abilities and talents before they hire you. This benefit works both ways — you get a client base from people you know. It is an effective way to "advertise" your services — and one that allows you to get clients who are already very comfortable with you before they hire you.

The first step is to review the current catalog of continuing education courses offered by local colleges, universities and other organizations that provide adult education classes in your community. Call and ask for a print catalog if they do not have course information at their website. Once you have reviewed their current list of courses, come up with some ideas for new courses. (They already have instructors for any courses that are in their catalog.)

Once you have an idea for a new course in mind, call the college or organization and ask to speak with whoever hires continuing education instructors. They will tell you what you need to do to apply.

Your Own Workshops or Seminars

While teaching continuing education courses can be rewarding, it normally takes months for a new course to be offered (and there's always the chance the continuing education program may decide not to offer it). If you'd like to start presenting courses right away, consider designing and giving your own workshops or seminars.

You will need to choose a date and time (evenings are usually best for businesspeople) and a location. You might approach a strategic partner (such as a business that sells supplies used in home or office organizing) about holding the seminar there. Or you could book a meeting room at a hotel or conference center.

You will then have to decide how much to charge. Consider making the fee comparable to continuing education courses offered in your community. Or it may be free if you are offering it in conjunction with a strategic partner.

If you are working with a strategic partner, they will likely market it to their customers. However, they will expect you to do some marketing yourself, and you will be responsible for getting registrations yourself if you hold it at another location. The following is from the *FabJob Guide to Become a Motivational Speaker*, which gives detailed advice on how to market a seminar.

When preparing your marketing materials, remember to focus on communicating all the benefits of attending. As well as the information, benefits of attending a seminar may include: a fun night out, a chance to network, or personal advice from an expert. The other items you might put in a brochure include:

- Who should attend

- When and where the seminar takes place

- The speaker's credentials

- Testimonials

- That enrollment is limited (mention if past seminars sold out)

- A call to action, such as "Register now"

• How to register, including your phone number and web address

Brochures with this information can also be used to market seminars to the public. The ideal brochure for a public seminar is one that can double as a poster (e.g. printed on one side of a colorful 8 1/2" x 11" sheet).

Preparing a Presentation

Organizing your thoughts is an important part of being able to speak effectively in front of a group. The best way to prepare a speech is to create an outline of your talk — and then work from that outline. A presentation outline template appears on the next page.

Effective speaking is not like learning monologues in a play in which you memorize every single word. Effective speakers know their topic and their ideas, plan a structure to present their ideas, and then practice speaking on each idea that they have outlined.

In the course of actually speaking, an audience member may ask a question or something unforeseen may happen. Successful speakers use an outline to allow them to stay on task, but at the same time adjust according to what is happening in the room.

Improving Your Speaking Skills

Our experts agree that public speaking opportunities are a business goldmine. And just like many people say that drinking coffee is an acquired taste, the same can be said of public speaking… you can develop a "taste" for it over time. And don't believe that old statistic that surfaces occasionally about how most people fear death less than speaking in front of a group. Like all public speakers will tell you, baby steps are the way to start.

Perhaps you will begin by getting up and introducing yourself and your business at networking meetings. Soon you will realize that you can hold your own while speaking before friends about your business. Next you might lead a discussion group on your subject — finally you will help run a small class on organization, and so on. No matter how you start, you will see that wearing the hat of the public speaker will increase your business.

Presentation Outline Template

"Ten Quick Organizing Solutions" *(10 minutes)*

Step 1: Introduction
Introduce yourself and your company. *(1 minute)*

Notes: _____

_____

_____

Step 2: Topic
Explain why you are speaking and your topic. For example: "I am here to talk to you today about ten easy steps for organizing. Before we are done, you will have ten quick ways to improve your organization today!" *(2 minutes)*

Notes: _____

_____

_____

Step 3: Talking Points
Write talking points or cues for ten organizational points. When you practice, keep points to about 30-45 seconds each.

- Point 1
- Point 2
- Point 3
- Etc.

Step 4: Conclusion
Sum it all up, thank your audience and end your presentation with your contact information. *(1 minute)*

Notes: _____

_____

_____

Learn From Others

There is nothing like watching a pro! Use opportunities in the groups you network in to see other public speakers in action. Take the time to record what you like and don't like about their performances. Think of each opportunity you have to watch someone else speak in public as a training ground for yourself and refining your own skills.

Talk shows are another excellent place to see superb public speakers in action. Most talk show hosts are polished public speakers, as are many of their guests. One important thing to watch is how a true professional handles a microphone.

Use the *Speaker Evaluation Form* that begins on the next page to evaluate the speakers you see. You can even bring it into a seminar and use it while you are listening as part of your note-taking. This way you will be able to remember the nuances of public speakers' performances and what you liked about their presentations.

Record Yourself at Home

Recording yourself using a video camera is an excellent way to get a sense of how you appear when you are speaking in front of a group. Use a tripod to secure the camera in one place, and place the camera so that the shot includes your whole body to observe any mannerisms you may be unaware of.

After you have created a tape, view it and critique yourself. See what mannerisms you have that are effective, and determine which you should limit. Look for speech mannerisms such as repeating words like "you know" or a sound like "um."

Set Up Speaking Parties

Successful public speakers say that nothing helps them improve more than good old-fashioned practice. Enlist your family members, neighbors, and friends to come to an "organization party" right in your own home. Use this time to give a presentation in front of people who know you and are supportive. If you meet people who are interested in public speaking, you can arrange to meet with them once a month and practice presentations together.

Speaker Evaluation Form

Date: _____

Speaker: _____

Presentation Title: _____

Hosting Organization: _____

For the questions below, please circle your response or write your answer on the lines.

Appearance:

1. Did the speaker's appearance add or detract from the presentation?   *Add   Detract*

2. Did the speaker dress appropriately for the group and situation?   *Yes   No*

3. What did you like or dislike about the speaker's appearance, and why?

   _____

   _____

   _____

Voice:

1. Could you hear the speaker?   *Yes   No*

2. Did the speaker articulate?   *Yes   No*

3. Did the speaker use a microphone?   *Yes   No*

4. Was it handled professionally?   *Yes   No*

5. What, if anything, could the speaker have done differently to improve his/her voice?

   _____

   _____

   _____

Poise:

1. Did the speaker seem confident?   *Yes   No*

2. Did the speaker appear comfortable?   *Yes   No*

3. Did you notice any signs of vocal nervousness or mannerisms? What were they?

_____

_____

_____

4. What, if anything, could the speaker have done differently to improve his/her level of poise?

_____

_____

_____

Command of Material:

1. Did the speaker have an organized presentation?   *Yes   No*

2. Did the speaker present the main ideas of the topic clearly?   *Yes   No*

3. Was the talk interesting?   *Yes   No*

4. Was the talk well-paced?   *Yes   No*

5. Was the presentation (check one):
   ❏ Too long
   ❏ Too short
   ❏ Timed about right

Props and Handouts:

1. Did the speaker use any props? If so, what were they?

_____

_____

2. Were the props helpful or distracting?   *Helpful   Distracting*

3. Did the speaker use handouts? What were they?

_____

_____

_____

4. Were the handouts helpful or distracting? *Helpful   Distracting*

General Impressions:

Please record your general impressions below.

_____

_____

_____

_____

_____

_____

Take an Acting Class

If you are very timid about public speaking you may find it useful to "play the role" of a speaker rather than be one. The subtle distinction will help you be more relaxed, and the acting exercises that you will learn in a beginning acting class are very enjoyable and extremely freeing. Most community colleges and community theaters have acting classes that are attended by people from all walks of life and all ages.

Join Toastmasters

The Toastmasters International group provides information and resources about public speaking to its members as well as a supportive community of people who are working to perfect their speaking skills just as you will be. Members offer each other constructive feedback and an audience. There are many Toastmasters groups across the United States and Canada. Membership in Toastmasters costs a one-time small fee and very reasonable semi-annual dues. Check your telephone directory or visit **www.toastmasters.org**.

Consider Learning PowerPoint

Way back when, all public speakers used easels that held a giant pad of paper and then wrote on the paper and flipped each page as they went along. Although many public speakers now use overhead projectors for audio-visual presentations, many other public speaker use presentation software to get a point across. PowerPoint, Microsoft's powerful presentation software, is based on the idea of an outline. There are bells and whistles that allow you to make quality presentation slides, which you can then use on an overhead or a presentation projector that hooks up to a computer.

Learn by Doing

There is no substitute in public speaking for just getting out there and trying it. After you have planned a short presentation, find somewhere to present it. Actually going and speaking before a group will give you more experience and confidence than any other kind of practice.

The added benefit of lots of practice is the reason you are doing it in the first place — speaking will get you and your business out in the public eye. People will associate you with the organizing services you provide and they will take your card.

> **TIP:** If you are at the beginning of your career as a professional organizer and you don't have anything to sell at your presentation, give away information at the back table and have a sign up sheet available for people who would like a free consultation. This will allow you to get instant leads!

Professional organizers interviewed for this guide told us that most of their business comes from referrals and word of mouth. You can get people talking about what you do by simply going and talking to them!

5.2.8 Other Marketing Techniques

Here are some additional marketing techniques you can consider matching to your target market. Note that with any kind of marketing you pay for, start small and have a way to measure results, such as a coupon code, or simply asking clients where they heard of you. This way you can fine-tune your marketing to include only what generates the most solid leads.

Traditional Advertising

Traditional advertising – buying space in media such as newspapers, magazines, radio and television – can be expensive and may not result in enough business to cover the advertising costs. If you choose to buy advertising, it will probably be most cost-effective to place ads in small local magazines or newspapers. The publications you advertise in will usually design your ad for an additional cost, and give you a copy of the ad to run in other publications.

You can also consider an ad or a listing in the local phone directory, but our experts advise that you thoroughly screen your potential clients first, or you may be wasting your time.

Internet Advertising

Some ways that you can market your business on the Internet include your own website, web rings that link you with other organizers and services, encouraging others to link to your site, and buying web browser ads so that every time someone searches on your keywords your ad comes up. You can find information about online advertising at search engine websites such as **www.google.com/ads**.

Tradeshows and Fairs

There are a wide variety of tradeshows and fair opportunities that a professional organizer can attend — either as an exhibitor, or even walking the tradeshow floor as a spectator armed with cards and conversation about your business in an informal way. At a tradeshow you have the ability to see and interact with many potential clients in the span of just a few hours.

Charitable Donations

If you can put yourself in the public eye in a positive light it will help your business. Many professional organizers give back to the community whenever possible. They help charities, or they donate their time or a portion of their sales income to charitable causes. Besides being a truly good thing to do, providing service to the community is good for professional organizers' business reputations. Look for ways in your community in which you can "give back" on behalf of your business.

5.3 Selling Your Services

When you hear the word "salesperson" what do you think of? Do you imagine a friendly, confident person who understands your needs and is dedicated to helping you get the services you want in a way that makes you comfortable and happy? Or do you think of someone pushy, dishonest, and rude?

If you answered "pushy, dishonest, and rude" you aren't alone. Many people have a bad impression of salespeople, but to run your organizing business, you will have to sell your services. The goal is to be the kind of salesperson you want to be – one who projects a friendly, confident, caring attitude – and truly helps their clients get what they really need.

From the moment your marketing efforts turn into leads – or opportunities for prospective clients – you'll need to know how to sell. In this section you will learn about:

- How you are your own marketing tool

- The sales process: from first call to the finished job

- Leads: where they come from and how to respond

- Telephone screening and sales

- The consultation: selling your services face-to-face

- Client materials: what your clients need to know before they buy

- Completing the work and getting paid

5.3.1 It All Starts With You

Professional organizers know that how they look and how they present themselves must inspire confidence in prospective clients. Making a good first impression quickly is an important part of making clients feel comfortable and eventually getting clients' business.

Consider what is known as the Ten Second Rule. (We have all done this!) You see someone new, and in the first few seconds you have an opinion about him or her. Before you have actually been introduced, even before you shake hands, or hear a person's name, you have an opinion. You have gathered facts and have formed an opinion — either positive or negative.

Professional organizers are interested in maintaining an image that reflects their professionalism. How they appear to their clients gives their clients confidence in them. For both women and men this means you need to pay attention to your grooming, clothing, behavior and attitude. While this might seem like pretty basic stuff, it is amazing how many people make mistakes that cost them client business.

Your Personal Appearance

How you dress when you are actually at work with a client will depend a lot upon what sort of job it is and what you are doing. In every specialty in the professional organizing marketplace you will find subtle variations in what is a normal look:

- If you go to companies you will want to appear corporately dressed.

- If you are organizing garages you will wear clothing and shoes that allow you to roll up your sleeves and get to work.

- If you are working with senior citizens you may choose to dress more conservatively than if you work mostly with young professionals.

Oddly enough, clothing should both convey a good impression and, by its very nature, be forgettable. It should simply be part of your package of professional presentation — it shouldn't take focus away from you, who you are, your attitude, or what you are saying.

Evaluate where you are today. If you were meeting yourself for the first time, would you feel relaxed and confident about the person you see? What do you need to do to create the image you want? The best thing to do is convey a professional image. Decide what that looks like for your geographic area and specialty, and dress the part.

Don't forget that your image extends beyond your person. Make sure your car gives potential clients the right impression. It doesn't have to be fancy, just clean, neat, and in good repair. The cars in the parking lot at the meeting of the Arizona chapter of NAPO the author of this guide attended were spotless on the outside and neat as pins inside.

Your Behavior

Anyone who watched the Austin Powers movies still laughs at the famous phrase, "Oh, behave!" Behavior slip-ups in the movies are the stuff of comedy, but behavior slip-ups in sales situations are the stuff of missed opportunity and lost clients. Here are some real-life things you may do that can cost you clients:

- Chewing gum

- Talking too loudly or too softly

- Taking unrelated cell phone calls

- Swearing

- Telling inappropriate jokes

- Not listening

- Smoking

- Nail-biting

- Bad breath

- Smell of alcohol

Becoming aware of your mannerisms, your behaviors, and your unconscious habits is a sometimes uncomfortable realization. Everyone has mannerisms that are part of who they are, it is just when those mannerisms become constant or magnified that they can become a problem. Think about your friends. Don't you know at least one person with a truly grating voice, or a phrase they always repeat? Being aware of your own mannerisms is an excellent way to begin to see yourself as others see you.

On the other hand, there are many positive ways you can express yourself to clients. You can let your own best qualities shine through, you can be charming and personable or friendly and caring — all things that clients like and remember. People like friendly business relationships — and the clients you work with as a professional organizer are no exception.

Consider the personal qualities that make you likable and memorable to others, or ask your friends to supply them for you. Let the great things about your own personality make building business relationships with clients not only good business, but a pleasure.

The Right Attitude

Selling is a learned skill that can be simple and natural. Selling doesn't have to be some high-pressure sales pitch that makes everyone un-comfortable. Try to keep the following "mental tips" in mind as you learn more about selling techniques:

1. Have a positive outlook about what you are selling, its value, and your ability to deliver it.

2. There is enough business for everyone, and enough for you to sustain your business.

3. Sell only to people who can legitimately use your services. Never sell to anyone who you know you can't help.

4. Everyone you meet has something of value for you. If it isn't a sale, it will be a contact, a referral, or more knowledge about how to do a better job selling to future clients.

5. Selling is about connecting with other human beings with integrity and friendliness. You don't have to be pushy, you only have to connect. It is a process of seeing how you can develop a positive working relationship with one another.

5.3.2 The Process

How do you take clients from mild interest or a phone call to paying clients? It's a matter of technique — sales technique. And like every other aspect of becoming a professional organizer, you can learn how to do it. The sales process is an easy process to follow once you know the steps. Look at the diagram below to see how the process moves naturally from one step to the next.

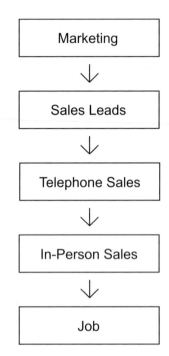

Marketing

As discussed earlier in this chapter, in this step you do what you need to do to get attention for your business in the marketplace. You network, you book speaking engagements, you get press, you advertise — whatever it takes to generate interest and excitement about your professional organizing business.

Sales Leads

Sales leads are the next step in the process. If you have done your marketing, you will see that pretty soon there are people who are interested in your business who will contact you or ask to be contacted. These are sales leads or potential clients.

Telephone Sales

Your first contact with clients will often be by phone. It is during this step that you "qualify" sales leads. This process allows you to determine whether or not you choose to move forward in the selling process and whether or not potential clients do as well. You need to successfully "sell" or "close" clients on seeing you in person for a consultation appointment.

In-Person Sales

In this step you sell your services to clients face-to-face. In-person sales will often take the form of free consultation appointments. You will be armed with your client materials and your portfolio of past work, and maybe a general idea of what the client's organization issues are. You will establish rapport, determine their needs, present your services in a way that is appropriate for them, and then close the sale.

The Job

This is the step you have been waiting for — when you actually get to show your talent and skill as a professional organizer. In this step you help clients transform their residential and business spaces or personal lives. After you are done you will receive payment, get clients' feedback, and possibly referrals.

Note that in rare cases you'll be able to move right to the job step without going through the process of a free consultation appointment, such as when you already have a personal connection with the client and a good idea of what their challenges are.

5.3.3 Sales Leads

To get paying clients you must identify prospective clients, known as sales leads. Leads generally come from the marketing activities you pursue, but you can get a lead in any situation in which someone finds out about your business and makes a decision to contact you, or asks to be contacted. The process of getting leads takes action steps such as the following:

- You give someone a business card

- Someone asks you to call them (a "strong" lead because they are requesting your call)

- You get a call regarding advertising or marketing you have done

- You get a call from a referral

- You get an email from someone who saw your website

Part of the process of determining which leads are the best ones to pursue is to "qualify" them. This means you get enough information from prospective clients so you can make the decision about whether they are likely enough to buy from you to pursue them as leads.

Once you get a lead, you want to qualify them by determining if they have the ability, the willingness, and the need to buy from you. For people to buy from you they must fit all three of those criteria. Once a lead is qualified, you can begin to sell them on your service.

5.3.4 Telephone Sales

Telephone sales are like "mini" sales appointments over the phone. You will go through shortened versions of the same steps you'll pursue in person to determine if you can help someone with their query. You will establish rapport, determine need, make a presentation of your services, and get the appointment.

Phone Rapport

Here are six easy ways to establish rapport over the phone with potential clients:

- Say hello and ask them how they are doing

- Mention the weather (Weather is a non-controversial topic!)

- Mention where you connected with them originally

- Mention a current event, or something interesting that is happening to you today

- React positively to something going on in the background of their conversation

- Be real, friendly, nonjudgmental and kind

Quick Needs Determination

The first thing you have to do with potential clients is to find out what they truly need. This is called "needs determination" and it is fairly simple. To determine need you must only do two things: you must ask clients what they need, and you must listen.

Ask them about their reason for calling you today, or asking to be called. Here are four questions to ask to get clients talking about their needs:

- How can I help you?

- Are you looking for help with home or office organization?

- What area of your home or office are you looking for help with?

- What's the most stressful thing about your current setup?

After a quick hello, many potential clients will want to ask you questions about your services and products. Answer them briefly, but then turn it around with a question about their needs. You don't want them to decide you can't help them without a fair chance to explain what you do.

Clients will usually tell you exactly what they need. They will tell you what is wrong and they will tell you what they would like to see changed. They will give you all the information you need to move to the next step in the sales process.

If potential clients ask questions, answer them only if you have enough information about their specific job to do so. Tell them you need to get more information before you make recommendations, during a face-to-face meeting. You must be able to tailor your services in a way that will fulfill clients' needs. If you can't, don't work with them. If you can, let them know you can.

Present Your Services

At this point in a telephone conversation, you need to move toward setting the client appointment by presenting your services. Make your presentation based on clients' specific situation. You might say something like:

"It sounds like your situation with your kids' schedules and your workload is getting overwhelming. I've studied time management, and I think I can help you find balance in your life with some techniques I've learned. Let's pick a time when we can sit down and really get a handle on what is making you feel so out of control."

Don't have a canned presentation that sounds like a broken record. Even if you have rehearsed your one-minute personal commercial and know it by heart, taking the time to address the client's needs will make them feel like you really listened to them. Save the commercial for people who ask what you do for a living.

If you only sell to clients based on their needs and what you have determined you can do to help them, not only will you make a lot of sales and have happy clients, but you will also enjoy selling, and you will do it with total honesty.

If they have agreed that your services can solve their problem, clients say yes, and you start setting appointments for work. Even if you don't end up taking a job or getting a client, you will have made a connection, which may turn into a referral or a future sale.

Get the Appointment

One excellent appointment-setting technique is called the "either/or" close. An either/or close is what is known as an assumptive close, which means you assume they want an appointment; it is just a matter of when.

When you are booking clients for appointments, give them options of things they can choose. Never say, "Do you want an appointment?" Say, "Would you like to have your free consultation Monday at 12:00 or Tuesday at 11:00?"

When to Say No

Especially with cold calls from people who know little about your service, you may find that you don't want to work with someone. In this case, explain that you cannot perform the job they need and get out of it gracefully. It may be because you know you don't have the skills needed. If this is the case, see if you can refer the lead to someone else.

Telephone Sales Form and Script

You can adapt this form and script for your own business, and then keep it by the phone for when opportunity knocks. Use the "conversation cues" to keep your sales pitch on track.

Contact's name: _____

Lead obtained from: _____

Organizational area client is looking for help in:

- ❏ Home
- ❏ Business
- ❏ Personal
- ❏ Other

Conversation Cue:

"Tell me about your current situation."

Notes: _____
_____
_____
_____

Conversation Cue:

"What would you like to change about the situation?"

Notes: _____
_____
_____
_____

Conversation Cue:

"I think I can help you, so let me tell you a little bit about how my service works. First, I come out to your location for a free, no-obligation consultation. This will give you a chance to meet me, and for me to get a first hand look at your (organizational dilemma).

This gives us a chance to talk in depth about how I can assist you and it gives me a chance to determine how long I anticipate the job will take and what exactly it will entail. Then you and I will have a chance to discuss the details, and if we are both comfortable we can set an appointment date and time for the job.

These consultations usually only take about a half-hour. I have an opening _____ at _____ or _____ at _____. Which one works better for you?"

Consultation Date: _____

Time: _____

Phone Number: _____

Meeting Address: _____

It could also be that you would like to work with them, but they aren't ready. If this is the case, place this lead in your "re-contact" file.

Very occasionally, it may be that you just have a funny feeling about the person on the other end of the phone. Always go with your gut feeling with a cold lead that doesn't feel right. Most professional organizers say they rarely or never have this situation, but in any situation where you will be going alone into someone's home you need to be mindful of your security.

5.3.5 In-Person Sales

"I recommend that new professional organizers offer a free consultation, which gives you the opportunity to have a 'face-to face' and build some rapport. It also gives you an opportunity to see a client's 'mess' and begin to formulate a plan."

— Ramona Creel, Professional Organizer

Professional organizers are usually willing to go out to clients' locations for a free consultation appointment. These appointments give them a chance to see their potential clients in person, and to get to understand the situation.

Here's the "secret": this free consultation appointment is actually a sales appointment. You should go prepared to give the clients all the information they will need to make a final decision on using your service, including contracts and your availability.

Client Materials

You will create a client presentation folder with materials to give clients during a face-to-face meeting. Purchase a presentation folder from an office supply store, and make copies of the documents you would like to include. Place these in the order you would like to present them to the client. Many presentation folders have a slot for you to insert your business card too.

You can include a file folder inside the presentation folder that you can take out and keep for yourself. Place the permanent files inside as you present the materials to clients, and make two copies of any document that you and a client sign so you have one for your permanent file. It looks professional, and lets you go back to your office with the pertinent materials in place for your own files.

The following are a list of suggested forms for your Client Presentation Folder. Note that some materials are to be left with the client, while others are meant for the client to fill out and you to keep.

A "Menu" of Services

It's a good idea to make a "menu" or list of your products and services for clients to follow along with as you speak. This helps them to understand what you offer, especially people who are visual learners. You can also include your brochure (see section 5.1.2).

A Rate Sheet

Most potential clients prefer to see something about price in writing. It can also explain the necessary provisos that you may have about minimum hours, hourly rate, special jobs, or special situational pricing. If you create a pricing document it doesn't have to be set in stone — you can even change and update this form from job to job if you want. A sample rate sheet appears in section 4.3.2.

Contract

Your contract is a letter or agreement that you and your clients sign to begin the process of working together. Your contract should spell out what services you will provide for the client, when you will provide them, as well as when and how you are to be paid.

Two sample contracts are included in section 4.3.3. As with all legal documents, you should have your attorney look over and approve your contract.

Work Schedule

This can also be a reminder card that clients can post somewhere in their houses, similar to the type used by doctor's offices. You can also state your cancellation policy on it. You can staple your copy of the work schedule to the folder to ensure that you have logged the appointment in your schedule or calendar.

A Bonus or "Thank-You"

First-time or potential clients also like it if you can provide them with some reading material about organizing. They like to have something that they can read themselves to get some preliminary information. There are a few ways to go about this. Consider including client assessments provided in section 3.2.1, or any other printed organizing information you would like to include. You can:

- Write something yourself – and if it's a reprint of a published article, so much the better – that lends you additional credibility. The ultimate organizational reference material would of course be a book you published. You can sell or give them a copy of this, depending upon your total number of hours billed with a client.

- Give them a tip book — as explained, many organizers make their own tip books, or you can buy one from another organizer.

- Give them a list of recommended organizing books. See the section 4.1.1 on how to compile booklists of both recently released books and library books on organizational topics.

Your Portfolio

A portfolio (a collection of samples of previous work, displayed attractively) is a useful sales and marketing tool. Having one allows you to carry your office with you, in a sense, and will vouch for the quality of your work with examples.

To put together your portfolio, you will need a portfolio or presentation book with clear plastic pages. Get a nice, new attractive one from an office supply store or art store. Remember, it will be the first thing clients will notice about your presentation and you want it to look like you value and are proud of your work. Inside you will include:

Organizing products from Mill's Pride: Deep Closet Organizer, Shoe Grid Organizer, Shelf Pack and 48" Shelves. Photo courtesy of Mill's Pride.

- Before-and after-photographs of your organizing projects

- Testimonials and letters of appreciation

- Articles you have written

- Press clippings featuring you or your business

- Evidence of certification or professional affiliation

- Awards you have won

- Copies of additional client materials

Every time you do a job you should ask the client's permission to take before-and-after pictures so you can document your results, and update your portfolio with only your best work. The more professional and glossy your photos look, the better. Make sure prints are large enough to see clearly.

If you are just getting started and haven't done any paid work before, you can still include before-and-after pictures of your own kitchen or bathroom or home office, or work you have done for friends. You can offer your family and friends free or discounted work in exchange for their agreement that they will let you take before-and-after pictures of the space you organize.

Any time you do an organizing job for anyone – even a close family member or friend – get a letter of reference about how much they enjoyed your work and how pleased they are with the results. Ask those who write references for you if they will agree to be contacted by potential clients as well. These testimonials will help you create a good reputation in the marketplace — and they will increase trust with potential clients.

The First Impression

Give yourself more than ample time to arrive for a consultation — nothing ruins a first impression more than tardiness. Verify your route, ask your potential clients for definite directions, and carry a map and cell phone in the car. (Remember to log your travel mileage for your taxes!)

While most professional organizers never have any problems with client appointments, when you enter a prospective client's home you should be cautious and use good sense. Always prescreen the potential client on the phone before going to their home for an appointment. Make sure that you leave your master schedule somewhere that you know your family can get to it.

Carry your cell phone with you. If you feel uncomfortable for any reason, excuse yourself and leave. Call your answering machine when you arrive in front of the prospective client to "tell your assistant" that you have arrived — mention the prospective client's name, address, and phone for your "master records." You can also call your next appointment in a potential client's presence and let them know your arrival time.

When you arrive, review your notes from your telephone screening and sales calls. If you took good notes you should be able to remember a lot about the potential clients and their particular needs. When you first come face to face, begin with a firm handshake and a smile, and make eye contact. You can say something positive, and review what you know about them in a friendly way.

Needs Assessment

After you have established rapport with potential clients it is time for the fact-finding part of an appointment. During needs determination you want to actively listen — and let clients tell you their stories in as much detail as you can get. Ask open-ended questions and listen (an open-ended question is one that can't be answered with a yes or no).

Part of your job is to figure out clients' abilities and skill levels before you begin. Teaching skills to those with natural talent is a different experience than teaching skills to those without it. A good organizer learns to recognize the skill and talent levels of clients before he or she helps them create systems and learn processes that will work for their individual strengths and weaknesses. Take notes as you go along.

Part of the needs determination may involve taking a look at the problem areas. For example, if a client wants help organizing his garage, go look at it, take pictures, and write down some notes. If it is a filing system in an office, take a tour and see the filing system in question. You can use the *Room Analysis Form* in section 3.4.4 for residential organizing, or use the *Workspace Organizational Assessment* in section 3.6.1 for business organizing.

Present Your Services and Close

As you go through, think about potential solutions and get ready to present your services in a manner that solves clients' organizational problems specifically. Clients want to know that you heard them, you understand what they need, and you have just the thing to solve their problems.

After a tour and information gathering, you will sit down and go over the documentation in the client presentation folder. This will help the clients choose what services they want and it will give you a chance to discuss your hourly rate, your minimum hours per appointment, and the terms of your contract, including confidentiality and your guarantee.

The last step of the appointment is the close. Closing is the sales term for getting the sale — and that you will start the work you have outlined in your work agreement. In many cases, once you have done the other steps of the appointment process, the best way to move to a close is to get out your calendar to book the job.

Then you finally get to do what you have been hoping to do since you first began reading this book — you get to start working with paying clients helping them organize their homes and businesses.

5.3.6 Creating a Winning Proposal

After meeting with the client, he or she may be interested in seeing a written proposal. A proposal is a written document, usually in the form of a letter, outlining what you propose to do for an organization.

If you have done an effective job of identifying the client's needs during the meeting, the proposal should simply put in writing what you agreed to during the meeting. However, you may occasionally be asked to prepare a proposal when a client is not seriously interested in doing business with you. So before you invest hours in preparing the proposal consider whether or not it is a good investment of your time.

Why Organizations Ask for Proposals

Sometimes the request for a proposal may come "out of the blue" from a client you haven't approached. The beginning professional organizer typically thinks this is great news. After all, why would they ask for a proposal if they were not interested? Actually, there are a number of reasons employers ask for proposals:

It May Be Necessary for the Job

In some cases, a proposal is necessary for the job. For example, many government departments require the decision-maker to review written proposals from several different prospects before a contract is awarded. They will often have formal RFP (request for proposal) guidelines for you to follow. Likewise, some large companies require written proposals.

If you pay attention to how they communicate with you, you should get a sense of how your proposal will be treated when it is received. Are they encouraging? Do they return your calls promptly? Do they sound positive about your chances? If the answer is "yes" and you want the job, it is probably worth your time to write the proposal. However, there may be times that writing a proposal will be a waste of your time and energy.

It May Be a "Brush Off"

Some clients find it difficult to say "no" and want to avoid a confrontation. They can delay saying no by having you submit a proposal. The client can then say it is "under review" until you either give up or they finally work up the courage to tell you they are not interested.

It May Be Used to Confirm a Hiring Decision

The most common reason some clients ask for proposals is because they want to have written comparisons of several consultants. Often, they have a "preferred" consultant, and the purpose of written proposals is to help them confirm their decision, or show their supervisor or a hiring committee that they have "shopped around."

> **TIP:** If you are the preferred consultant you will know it. The client will have discussed the project with you in detail, and you will have reached a tentative agreement to do the work. They will explain that their regulations require them to review written proposals and may even assure you that it will be "just a formality."

If you are the preferred supplier and you want the job, then it is worth your time to put together a proposal confirming the details you have discussed with the clients. Otherwise, your time might be better spent focusing on clients who are seriously interested in you.

Responding to a Request For Proposal

If the client has a formal request for proposal (RFP) process, you will use that as the guideline in preparing your proposal. When you submit your proposal, you are making a "bid" to do the work. A typical RFP is a document that provides information about the organization, their needs, what they require in a proposal, and specific instructions for submission of the proposal.

You should expect to sell your company's suitability to provide organizing services, your fees and any other pertinent information. Here is an example of the type of information that might be expected in a proposal:

- A description of your company

- Demonstration of your capability to provide organizing services

- A proposed timetable

- A fixed price quotation

- Specific resources (such as employees) that you will assign to the project

- References from organizations you have done similar work for

- An explanation of how you will measure results

The bid process may also require you to make an oral presentation. The organization requesting the RFP will usually hold a session (sometimes called a bidding meeting) for interested parties (professional organizers and other suppliers) to attend to learn more about the project before submitting their response to the RFP. This is the time to ask questions and elicit clear answers. The more clearly you understand the goals and purpose of the project, the better your chances of being the successful bidder.

The client may not be obligated to award the contract to the "lowest cost" bidder. Instead, they may make their decision based on a number of factors, including the company's previous experience with similar projects.

A number of companies specialize in writing proposals. You can find them by doing a web search for "writing proposals" and "contract." An excellent resource is Deborah Kluge's webpage with links on proposal writing and government contracting at **www.proposalwriter.com/ links.html**

5.3.7 On the Job

From the moment you book a job and take a look at clients' situations during their consultation appointments, you are undoubtedly starting to brainstorm. Now is the time when you should plan your attack and decide what you are going to do to help your new clients solve their organizational problems.

Have a Plan

> *"New organizers… need to ask themselves ahead of time, 'What kind of "stuff" do I expect to see, and what kind of categories do I expect to see?' so they can start to break things into categories when they are with the client."*
>
> — Ramona Creel, Professional Organizer

You should spend some time planning ahead so you can go into appointments with new clients ready to move forward with self-assurance and confidence. Just like a teacher might plan lessons or a coach might plan plays for a team to practice, you should decide ahead of time what you will do in your time with clients. You can use the forms and worksheets throughout Chapter 3 to help you and your clients prepare a plan.

Tips for On-the-Job Success

- Call a day or two ahead of time to confirm your appointment.

- Arrive on time.

- Bring your assessment notes so you have a definite plan.

- Know your clients' organizing priorities and tackle tasks accordingly.

- Work at each client's pace. Don't try to schedule too much work for one session.

- Clients are individuals and will have different concerns and different lives. Treat their differences with respect.

- Respect clients' information and privacy.

- Let your clients be the decision makers. You can advise, counsel and teach, but you can't control.

- Be upbeat and positive about what you accomplish each appointment. Make appointments pleasant and fun for your clients.

- Offer support and encouragement.

Getting Feedback

After a job is completed you will want to get feedback from your clients. Getting feedback tells you what kind of job you are doing and gives you information you can use to improve your services.

> **TIP:** Make sure to get back in touch with previous clients on a regular basis, first to follow up several weeks after your job, and then periodically for re-order business. And make sure to ask for referrals. Leave everyone you work for several cards and ask them to refer their friends to you.

There are a variety of ways to get client feedback. The first and perhaps most obvious way is to ask for it. You can use a client feedback form that you give clients after the completion of a job, seminar, or class. A sample form is shown on the facing page.

Another option is to create a customer feedback link on your website so past customers can log on and fill out a form online. Check out Chris McKenry's Client Testimonial Section on his website for his business, Get it Together LA! at **www.getittogetherla.com/clientreviews.php**.

Client Feedback Form

Your Name: _____

What service or product did you purchase?

_____

_____

What dates did we work with you? _____

		Poor			Excellent
1.	What was your overall level of satisfaction with the job performed for you?	1	2	3	4

2. Please rate us on the following attributes:

	Poor			Excellent
Punctuality	1	2	3	4
Value	1	2	3	4
Friendliness	1	2	3	4
Professionalism	1	2	3	4
Technical knowledge	1	2	3	4
Response time	1	2	3	4
Integrity	1	2	3	4
Follow through	1	2	3	4

3. How well did we understand your organizational goals and needs?

_____

_____

_____

4. Would you use our services again?   Yes   No

5. Will you refer your friends and family to us?   Yes   No

6. Is there any way we could improve our service?

_____

_____

_____

There are two important reasons for you to actively pursue client feedback. First, clients are the best people to tell you where you need improvement, especially if you make the feedback process something that isn't stressful for them.

Secondly, clients are your best source of testimonials — people who have hired you and who have come away from the experience satisfied are good advertising for you. Ask clients if you have their permission to quote their positive comments in your portfolio, or on your website.

5.4 Success and Change

"You always want to be learning, and making sure you grow in your profession."

— Brenda Clements, Professional Organizer

Wicker 3 Drawer Chest from Stacks and Stacks.
Photo courtesy of Stacks and Stacks.

Success as a professional organizer isn't something you arrive at one day. It is a continual process of communicating effectively, acting with integrity in the marketplace, keeping your commitments, and doing a good job at what you do.

Once you are working as a professional organizer, you have clients, you complete jobs for them, and you get paid for your services, how do you measure and refine your success?

You can use the following indicators as a road map to improve and refine what you do. If you find one area that needs improvement, use this as information to help you redefine and change what you do in that area so you see the kind of results you want. You can make a difference simply by assessing where you are today and moving forward with a revised plan.

5.4.1 Profitability

The first way to measure business success is profit. Are you making money as a professional organizer? The best way to see if all your plans and everything you have implemented are successful is the bottom line. Take a look at the things you do to generate business profits and ask yourself questions like:

- Am I charging enough or too much?

- Am I as busy with paying jobs as I want to be?

- What is my lead-to-job ratio? (i.e. how many leads turn into paying clients?)

- How much money am I making annually after I subtract my costs?

Answer these questions to determine how you can refine your process. Do you need to get more leads? Maybe you are not networking enough. Do you work a lot but still feel you aren't making enough? Maybe you charge too little. Are you seeing a lot of potential clients for consultations but not closing the deal? Maybe you need to work on your presentation or your closing skills.

5.4.2 Evaluating Your Results

A powerful tool to measure your success is referrals from your clients. If your clients are happy, they will tell their friends. The more referral business you have, the better job you are doing with your clients.

Take a look at the things you do to generate goodwill with clients and ask yourself:

- Are your customers satisfied with the work you do?

- Do you have any trouble collecting payment?

- Are you getting a lot of referral and word-of-mouth business?

- Do you get positive feedback from clients in writing?

- Do you feel like your rapport is positive with your clients, even after the work is done?

- Do clients you have worked for before call you again for other jobs?

Answer these questions to determine how you can improve your relationship with clients. Do your clients seem unhappy? Maybe you are saying you will do more for them than you actually deliver, or maybe your contracts or work agreements aren't clear.

Think about if you are providing enough value for clients. Do clients only use you once? Call back clients you have worked with in the past and review their client feedback form with them.

Are you having trouble getting paid? Make sure you are communicating the cost of your services both verbally and in writing before you start. Are you getting fewer referrals than you think you should? Make sure you ask clients for referrals and provide them with extra business cards.

5.4.3 Your Recognition

Getting some recognition for what you do not only feels good, but also means that you are getting a positive reputation in the marketplace. There are a number of ways to see how your "approval rating" is. Take a look at the things you do to receive recognition in the marketplace, and ask yourself:

- Are you getting the word out to the press via press releases?

- Are you getting your articles published?

- Are you being asked for interviews?

- Have people in the industry heard of you and it is positive?

- Have you received any community recognition through your business networks?

- Do organizations and groups ask your business to be involved in civic, community, or industry events?

- Are you getting repeat speaking engagements?

Answer these questions to determine how you can improve your reputation in the marketplace. Do you have the reputation you want? Maybe you simply need to drum up more excitement about your business.

Are you getting any negative feedback about your business? If you are, try to find out exactly what it is and where it generated, and try to problem-solve in that area, with the right person.

Does there seem to be a lack of interest in your business? Maybe you need to really pump up your public relations and get yourself and your business into the spotlight more often.

5.4.4 Implementing Change

Implementing change is an important part of your ongoing success. Being open to the idea that you can improve a process or a situation is easy for a professional organizer to understand because it is the idea that is the very basis of why many people become organizers in the first place — you like to change things so they work better and so that you see better results.

Once you have an idea about what needs to change to improve and finesse your business results, it is up to you to make a plan and implement the changes. Then, once again, you reassess and move forward. Assessment and change in business is a cyclical thing — each time you see problems and make improvements, you reach a higher level of success.

6. Conclusion

"I don't think I could ever do anything else — I really enjoy it. You meet the nicest people. There is always something different—you do one thing and then you move on to something different with your next client. They're so appreciative. They thank you inside and out."

— Brenda Clements, Professional Organizer

This is the final chapter in the FabJob Guide to Become a Professional Organizer. Hopefully, this is also the beginning of your new career: helping people live organized lives that give them the time and space to truly be happy and successful.

As you have read the pages of this book you have seen that you can take your talent for organizing and make a lucrative, truly helpful business that will impact the world for good, all while giving you the freedom to do what you love the best—organize. Never lose sight of the valuable service that professional organizers provide. Without you, people would spin into chaos, mismanagement, financial devastation, and family unhappiness, just because they don't know how to create and follow organized systems. You will give people the freedom to focus on what they truly value in life without stress, anxiety, and disorder weighing them down.

We sincerely hope you have enjoyed it and will refer back to it frequently as you progress in your career. We wish you great success as a professional organizer, and in all areas of your life.

6.1 Profiles of Successful Organizers

Organizers all have their own stories that led them to the business of professional organizing, and their own methodologies and procedures for getting clients' homes and workspaces from messy to magnificent.

The professional organizers interviewed for this book come from all areas of the U.S. and Canada and specialize in a vast variety of different services. All of them have found approaches that work for them and have created businesses that highlight their strengths. All of them are expert at what they love to do, were incredibly professional, extremely forthcoming, and happy to share their thoughts about the business they love. Here are some profiles of these experts so you can learn a bit more about what they do.

6.1.1 Arranging It All

Barry Izsak, owner of Arranging It All in Austin, Texas, calls his business a "one-stop shop." His businesses motto is "No job is too tall or too small — we do it all!" He considers himself an organization generalist with his business doing everything from creating systems in corporations, small business, and home offices, to all aspects of residential organization, especially closets. Barry's company even handles some of the construction elements of closets.

Barry is the current president of NAPO, and a sought-after speaker for corporations, businesses, and other groups around the country. He is currently writing a book about closet organization. Barry's business offers professional coaching for beginning professional organizers to help them get their own businesses off the ground. Visit his website at **www.arrangingitall.com**.

6.1.2 Business Organizing Solutions

Carol Halsey, owner of Business Organizing Solutions in Wilsonville, Oregon, runs a business that would not have been a possibility even ten years ago — she does her business exclusively by Internet and over the telephone. A business professional with an extensive background in the corporate world, Carol spends much of her time with clients in telephone consulting appointments. Carol says that she has spent so much time helping clients with time management, work flow, and office organization that she can now envision what is on a client's desk in her mind's eye without actually needing to see it!

Carol's website at **www.pilestofiles.com** is packed full of information, and she has written a variety of articles, reports, and a tip book which she sells to organizers who don't have time or the inclination to write one themselves. She finds that her writing not only generates income as a product she sells, but also serves as an excellent marketing tool.

6.1.3 Complete Organizational Services

Brenda Clements, owner of Complete Organizational Services in Glendale, Arizona, is a veteran organizer in the Phoenix area specializing in residential downsizing for seniors.

A Canadian transplant, she is a member of both POC and NAPO. She has served on the Arizona chapter board of NAPO for the last 4 years, including a term as president of the chapter.

In her specialty she works almost exclusively with seniors who are moving from larger homes into retirement homes or facilities. It gratifies Brenda that many of her clients come to think of her as a daughter as she helps them make difficult and emotional decisions about what to take from their homes of many years into their new environments.

Brenda spends a lot of her time networking with the various retirement facilities that her clients move to and gets the layout of the apartments in advance so she can assist them every step of the way. Her company's website is **www.complete-organizer.com**.

6.1.4   Get It Together LA!

Chris McKenry is the owner of the Los Angeles-based Get it Together LA! Chris has spent the last two or three years aggressively marketing his business and getting the word out about who he is and what Get It Together LA! can do for clients in his market. Chris' experience working in a family-owned corporation in the Midwest gave him the business know-how to put his company on the map in his new industry quickly.

Chris says, "When I am not with a client, I am doing something to market my business. I am either getting out there or figuring out how I can get out there." Chris specializes in organizing for both homes and offices and often appears as a public speaker. And because he works in the Los Angeles area, Chris works with a number of clients in entertainment-related industries. His website is **www.GetItTogetherLA.com**.

6.1.5   OnlineOrganizing.com

Ramona Creel, owner of OnlineOrganizing.com in Atlanta, Georgia, is a busy organizer who considers herself a generalist. She began her organizing career in the late 1990s and realized around the year 2000 there was a real lack of information on the Internet not only about organizing, but also for professional organizers who needed help getting information to get their businesses started.

Ramona has put together a website at **www.onlineorganizing.com** that is full of referral links, information, and products that professional organizers can use as a resource. She has also written a set of training modules on becoming a professional organizer.

Ramona sees clients all over the southeastern United States and finds with the success of her physical and digital businesses that she is really running two busy and successful entities. She has been interviewed for radio, written extensively, and is always on the lookout for ways to make her website more complete. She was the winner of the NAPO Organizer's Choice Award for Best Organizing Service for 2003-2005.

6.1.6 Organize Me 101

Laurene Livesey Park is the owner of Organize Me 101 in Ontario, Canada. Her focus is residential and family organizing and she brings a wealth of experience to her specialty, including a Bachelor of Applied Science Degree in Family Studies from the University of Guelph. She has honed her home organization skills through eight family moves in the first ten years of her marriage.

Laurene has written a tip book called *Havoc to Harmony at Home* with co-author Karen Sencich. She has also developed a product called *Steps to Success for Professional Organizers*, which she co-authored with Sencich to give professional organizers a boost up in the business. You can find it at her website at **www.organizeme101.com**.

Laurene is the past president of Professional Organizers in Canada (POC). She is also a speaker and workshop facilitator.

6.1.7 Student Success Services

Marcy Tanner, owner of Studet Success Services in Phoenix, Arizona, brings a very interesting background to her business as a professional organizer specializing in residential — she is a school psychologist.

Marcy concentrates her efforts as an organizer working with families, especially parents with children, who need help with homework organization and other time management skills that affect the young. Marcy specializes in helping parents create an atmosphere and a program that not only helps children learn the organizational skills necessary to take control of their schedules and responsibilities early on, but also that serve them for life as they become competent adults.

Marcy's wealth of experience working with children as a school psychologist has lead her to develop her career as a consultant and speaker. She is a charter member of NAPO Arizona.

6.1.8 Organized for Success

Karen Ussery of Phoenix, Arizona, is a ten-year veteran in the organizing industry. Karen works in home business, small business, and corporate organization and says she works with people "running a small business on a card table in their dining room all the way to Fortune 500s."

Karen focuses on business organizing, but also does business as a professional coach for new organizers who want to hire a mentor. Karen was the founder and past president of the Arizona Chapter of NAPO. Her company's website is **www.organizedforsuccess.com**.

6.1.9 R R Hird & Company

When Rozanne Hird of introduces herself you will be sure to hear her say, "I do Windows!" This doesn't mean that she is ready to visit her clients armed with Windex — she is actually a computer consultant with more than 10 years in the industry.

Rozanne specializes in training her clients to make sense of the data on their desk and laptops as well as learn how to effectively network the data that they need between their PDAs and their primary workstations. Rozanne specializes in database management and training clients to use ACT!, powerful contact management software which keeps track of contacts, calendar, and emails that she calls "a database on steroids."

Rozanne is a contributing member of a variety of different business and civic organizations. Based in Phoenix, Arizona, she serves as an officer in NAPO, Arizona. Her website is **www.rrhird.com**.

6.2 Local NAPO and POC Contact Info

6.2.1 NAPO Local Chapters

Arizona
1097 E. Butherus Drive
Scottsdale, AZ 85255
Phone: (602) 203-0463
www.napo-az.com

California – Los Angeles
10573 W Pico Blvd, PMB 134
Los Angeles, CA 90064
Phone: (213) 486-4477
www.napola.org

California – San Diego
P.O. Box 1824
La Jolla, CA 92038
Phone: (619) 687-7207
www.naposandiego.com

California –
San Francisco Bay Area
PO Box 895
Millbrae, CA 94030
Phone: (415) 281-5681
www.napo-sfba.org

Colorado
159-7476 E. 29 Avenue
Denver, CO 80238
Phone: (303) 388-3902
www.napocolorado.org

Connecticut
61 Chamberlain Highway
Suite 261
Kensington, CT 06037
info@napoct.com
www.napoct.com

Georgia
180 Worthington Drive
Marietta, GA 30068
Phone: (770) 579-9866
www.napogeorgia.com

Illinois – Chicago
PO Box 42777
Evergreen Park, IL 60805-0777
Phone: (312) 409-5523
www.napo-chicago.org

Michigan
PO Box 1347
Novi, MI 48376
Phone: (810) 348-1772
http://mi-napo.home.comcast.net

Minnesota
3500 Vicksburg Lane North, #168
Plymouth, MN 55447-1333
Phone: (612) 339-1331
www.mnnapo.org/info/info.htm

Missouri
75 W. Glenwood Lane
Saint Louis, MO 63122
Phone: (314) 220-7346

New England
270-321 Walnut Street
Newtonville, MA 02460-1927
Phone: (617) 335-1111
www.napo-newengland.com

New Jersey – Northern
PO Box 226
Englewood, NJ 07631
Phone: (201) 248-5208

New York
459 Columbus Ave, Ste 210
New York, NY 10024
Phone: (212) 439-1088
www.napo-ny.net

North Carolina
PO Box 1086
Morrisville, NC 27560
Phone: (919) 345-2846
www.naponc.org

Ohio
105-1280 W. 5 Avenue
Columbus, OH 43212
ttjones@columbus.rr.com

Oregon
PO Box 820042
Portland, OR 97282
Phone: (503) 768-5445
info@oregonnapo.com
www.oregonnapo.com

Pennsylvania – Philadelphia
22 Leopard Rd.
Berwyn, PA 19312
Phone: (610) 687-7207
www.napo-gpc.org

Pennsylvania – Pittsburgh
PO Box 11611
Pittsburgh, PA 15228
Berwyn, PA 19312
Phone: (412) 344-3252
www.napopittsburgh.org

Tennessee
PO Box 17431
Memphis, TN 38187-0431

Texas — Dallas/Fort Worth
PMB 237
376-2436 S. I-35E
Denton, TX 76205-4900
www.dfworganizers.com

Texas — Houston
6124 Hwy 6 N., #118
Houston, TX 77084
Phone: (713) 589-3364
www.napohouston.com

Washington D.C.
PO Box 7301
Arlington, VA 22207-0301
Phone: (202) 362-6276
www.dcorganizers.org

Wisconsin
PO Box 1903
Waukesha, WI 53187-1903
Phone: (262) 524-0889
www.napo-wi.com

6.2.2 POC Chapters

Atlantic Canada
Halifax, NS
Phone: (902) 479-0105
tipstoolstechniques@ns.sympatico.ca

**British Columbia –
Lower Mainland**
Vancouver, BC
Phone: (604) 813-8189
info@outofchaos.ca

Calgary
Phone: (403) 451-8159
organizingmatters@shaw.ca
www.organizingmatters.ca

Edmonton
Phone: (708) 437-8837
cluttercutter@telus.net

Halton-Peel
Phone: (902) 452-7674
neatspaces@cogeco.ca

Huron Shores
London, ON
Phone: (519) 472-9585, ext. 3
2margarita@rogers.com

Montreal
Phone: (514) 5757949
neira@espacebrillant.com

Ottawa
organizer@aroundtoit.biz

South-Western Ontario
Cambridge, ON
pts@gto.net

Toronto
Phone: (416) 593-1053
toronto@organizersincanada.com

Vancouver Island
Victoria, BC
Phone: (250) 389-0515
info@simplicity-by-design.com

Western Canada (SK/MB)
Winnipeg, MB
Phone: (204) 797-8480
info@spacetime.ca

6.3 More Resources

Here is a selection of websites and suppliers of organizing products and services. Additional websites and suppliers can be found in the appropriate sections of this guide.

Organizing Products

- *Cable Organizer.com*
  www.cableorganizer.com

- *California Closets*
  Call 800.274.6754
  www.calclosets.com

- *Mill's Pride*
  www.millspride.com

- *Organize-It — Plastic Storage*
  www.organizes-it.com/plastic.php

- *Smart Furniture*
  www.smartfurniture.com/shop/

- *Stacks and Stacks*
  www.stacksandstacks.com

Goal and Time Management

- *BusinessTown.com: Time Management Advice — Small Business Advice*
  www.businesstown.com/time/time.asp

- *Day-Timer Planners*
  www.daytimer.com

- *Franklin Covey.com*
  www.franklincovey.com

- *MyGoals.com*
  www.mygoals.com

Organizational Resources for Business

- *About.com — Basic Email Management*
  **http://sbinfocanada.about.com/cs/management/qt/
  email1.htm**

- *Creating a Project Management Plan*
  http://personal.ecu.edu/toveyj/projmgmt/home.html

Man's closet organized with products from Mill's Pride's Home Organization Product Catalog.
Photo courtesy of Mill's Pride.

- *Rules of Data Normalization*
  www.datamodel.org/NormalizationRules.html

- *PMI — Project Management Institute*
  www.pmi.org

Organizing Software

- *About.com — Top Five Time Tracking Software Programs*
  http://sbinfocanada.about.com/cs/software/tp/timetracking.htm

- *Collection Catalog Software*
  www.collectorz.com

Clutter and Chronic Disorganization

- *ADD/ADHD Online Support Group*
  www.adders.org

- *Clutter and Organizing Links*
  http://user.cybrzn.com/~kenyonck/add/Links/links_categories_clutter.html

- *National Study Group on Chronic Disorganization*
  (Has a certification program, teleconferences, events and other information.)
  www.nsgcd.org

Services

- *1-800-Got-Junk? — Junk Removal*
  www.1800gotjunk.com

- *Freecycle*
  (A network where you can give away things you no longer need to local people who come and pick them up.)
  www.freecycle.org

- *Trashbusters.com — Garbage and Rubbish Hauling Service*
  www.trashbusters.com

Feng Shui

- *The Feng Shui Directory*
  www.fengshuidirectory.com

- *World of Feng Shui Magazine*
  www.wofs.com

Organizing Forms

- *All Free Printables — Checklists*
  www.allfreeprintables.com/checklists/index.shtml

- *All Free Printables — To Do Lists*
  www.allfreeprintables.com/checklists/to-do-lists.shtml

- *The Frugal Shopper — Free Printables*
  www.thefrugalshopper.com/printables.shtml

- *Main Street Mom — Your Printable Lists*
  http://mainstreetmom.com/print/index.htm

- *OrganizedHome.com: Free Printable Planner Forms*
  www.organizedhome.com/printable/index.php/cat/501

- *SmartDraw — Easy Business Forms*
  www.smartdraw.com/specials/forms.asp?id=35917

Business Links and Resources

- *BizOffice.com — Small and Home-Based Business Forms*
  (More than 500 business form examples including contracts, proposals, confidentiality agreements and more.)
  www.bizoffice.com

- *CanadaOne — Canada's Small Business Source Online*
  www.canadaone.com

- *Entrepreneur.com — Starting and Growing a Small Business*
  www.entrepreneur.com

Tell Us What You Think

Would you like to share your thoughts with other FabJob readers? Please contact us at **www.FabJob.com/feedback.asp** to tell us how this guide has helped prepare you for your dream career. If we publish your comments on our website or in our promotional materials, we will send you a gift certificate for 50% off your next purchase of a FabJob guide.

The FabJob Newsletter

Get valuable career advice for **free** by subscribing to the FabJob newsletter. You'll receive insightful tips on:

- How to break into the job of your dreams or start the business of your dreams

- How to avoid career mistakes

- How to increase your on-the-job satisfaction and success

You'll also receive discounts on FabJob guides, and be the first to know about upcoming titles. Subscribe to the FabJob newsletter at **www.FabJob.com/signup_site.asp**.

More Fabulous Books

Find out how to break into the "fab" job of your dreams with FabJob career guides. Each 2-in-1 set includes a print book and CD-ROM.

Get Paid to Decorate

Imagine having a rewarding high paying job that lets you use your creativity to make homes and businesses beautiful and comfortable. **FabJob Guide to Become an Interior Decorator** shows you how to:

- Teach yourself interior decorating (includes step-by-step decorating instructions)
- Get 10-50% discounts on furniture and materials
- Create an impressive portfolio even if you have no previous paid decorating experience
- Get a job with a retailer, home builder or other interior design industry employer
- Start an interior decorating business, price your services, and find clients

Get Paid to Shop

Imagine having a creative high-paying job shopping for housewares, gifts, or almost anything else you love to shop for. In the **FabJob Guide to Become a Personal Shopper** you will discover:

- Step-by-step instructions for personal shopping from identifying what people want to finding the best products and retailers
- How to get discounts on merchandise
- How to prevent purchasing mistakes
- How to get a job as a personal shopper for a boutique, department store or shopping center
- How to start a personal shopping business, price your services, and find clients

Visit www.FabJob.com to order guides today!

Does Someone You Love Deserve a Fab Job?

Giving a FabJob® guide is a fabulous way to show someone you believe in them and support their dreams. Help them break into the career of their dreams with the ...

- FabJob Guide to **Become a Bed and Breakfast Owner**
- FabJob Guide to **Become a Business Consultant**
- FabJob Guide to **Become a Caterer**
- FabJob Guide to **Become a Celebrity Personal Assistant**
- FabJob Guide to **Become a Children's Book Author**
- FabJob Guide to **Become an Event Planner**
- FabJob Guide to **Become an Etiquette Consultant**
- FabJob Guide to **Become a Fashion Designer**
- FabJob Guide to **Become a Florist**
- FabJob Guide to **Become a Human Resources Professional**
- FabJob Guide to **Become an Interior Decorator**
- FabJob Guide to **Become a Makeup Artist**
- FabJob Guide to **Become a Massage Therapist**
- FabJob Guide to **Become a Model**
- FabJob Guide to **Become a Motivational Speaker**
- FabJob Guide to **Become a Public Relations Consultant**
- FabJob Guide to **Become a Super Salesperson**
- FabJob Guide to **Become a Wedding Planner**
- **And dozens more fabulous careers!**

Visit FabJob.com for details and special offers